A VISITOR'S GUIDE TO

the Literary South

TRISH FOXWELL

COUNTRYMAN PRESS
WOODSTOCK, VERMONT

This book is lovingly dedicated to my parents, who inspired me to lead a creative and adventurous life, and my grandparents, Bappy and John Myers, for their southern heritage and illuminating stories.

So we beat on, boats against the current, borne back ceaselessly into the past.

— F. SCOTT FITZGERALD, *The Great Gatsby*

Interior photographs by the author unless otherwise specified
Book design and composition by Eugenie S. Delaney

Published by The Countryman Press, P.O. Box 748, Woodstock, VT 05091
Distributed by W. W. Norton & Company, Inc., 500 Fifth Avenue, New York, NY 10110

Library of Congress Cataloging-in-Publication Data are available.

A Visitor's Guide to the Literary South
ISBN 978-1-58157-149-3

Printed in the United States of America

10 9 8 7 6 5 4 3 2 1

CONTENTS

INTRODUCTION

The happiness and serenity of the South disconcerted him. He had felt good in the North because everyone else felt so bad. . . . The South was at home. . . . They had everything the North had and more. They had a history, they had a place redolent with memories, they had good conversation. . . . They had the best of victory and defeat.
——WALKER PERCY, *The Last Gentleman*

WHAT IS IT ABOUT THE AMERICAN SOUTH that has produced and inspired such a rich repository of literature? To quote Walker Percy again, maybe it's "because [the South] lost the War." But perhaps the reasons go much deeper. Storytelling on verandas on breezy summer evenings is an important daily pastime. Telling a good story is, after all, every southerner's birthright.

The South is a region defined not only by its geography but also by the powerful literary voices that have emerged on its horizon. William Faulkner, Eudora Welty, Tennessee Williams, Thomas Wolfe, Margaret Mitchell, and countless others have sculpted their creativity in this mysterious and unique domain.

To deepen our appreciation for and understanding of the literary South is to explore the haunts, havens, and homesteads of the writers who lived and wrote here—to touch the landscape, if you will, that touched them, to experience the places that provided the settings for their lives and creative imaginings.

Mississippi is clearly Faulkner country, and the river with the same name decidedly all Twain's. New Orleans with its riotous temperament and streetcar named Desire is Tennessee Williams's town; few can dispute that Key West with its neon-lit backdrop is the domain of Ernest Hemingway. Virginia played a key role in Edgar Allan Poe's development as a writer, and growing up in Knoxville provided inspiration for Tennessean James Agee's novel *A Death in the Family.*

Although the familiar figures surfaced while I was researching this book in the South, other noteworthy names came to the forefront: Stephen Crane, Carson McCullers, F. Scott and Zelda Fitzgerald, Alice Walker,

Eugene O'Neill, Marjorie Kinnan Rawlings, and Sherwood Anderson all left their mark on the region, as evidenced in the South's vast number of literary landmarks.

This book does not seek to be comprehensive in its coverage. My objective was to focus on authors who left a significant imprint, and on places where travelers can immerse themselves in environments of literary significance.

Viewing the grand ballroom at Louisville's Seelbach Hotel that figured in Fitzgerald's *The Great Gatsby,* gazing out at the Florida scrub country that became the setting for Marjorie Kinnan Rawlings's *The Yearling,* and walking through Thomas Wolfe's childhood home in Asheville—which became *Look Homeward, Angel*—inspired me to write *Visitor's Guide to the Literary South.* In these pages now you'll find all the information you need to explore the Monroeville County Courthouse at the center of Harper Lee's *To Kill a Mockingbird;* peer inside the tiny apartment on Peachtree Street in storied Atlanta where Margaret Mitchell wrote *Gone with the Wind;* visit the Daytona lighthouse that figures in the dramatic exploits of Stephen Crane; and walk through Flannery O'Connor's childhood home in Savannah.

This book is organized alphabetically by state. Listings provide contact information if you'd like further information. "Literary Lodging" sidebars scattered throughout the book alert you to accommodations having literary or historical significance. To overnight in a place where a beloved author visited, stayed, or lived, or that figures prominently in his works, or that simply captures her era, adds to any literary pilgrimage. "Excursions and Diversions" sidebars point out special attractions and nearby sites of interest to literary travelers.

It is my hope that *Visitor's Guide to the Literary South* will inspire you to reacquaint yourself with—or pick up for the first time—the works of the authors discussed here as you explore the fascinating landmarks of the literary South. After all, no literary journey is complete without a good book.

CHAPTER
1

𝒜LABAMA

LABAMA'S HISTORY READS LIKE A COMPELLING NOVEL.
Spotlighted in the 1960s as a hotbed for the civil rights movement, the heart of Dixie has struggled carefully with its past in
redefining its present. Its dramatic history continues to linger over its landscape. Selma, the Montgomery bus boycott, and the heroic efforts of Rosa
Parks as well as those of Martin Luther King and his courageous crusades
are images forever etched in the minds of most Americans.

Alabama was discovered by Hernando de Soto, who led an an expedition here in 1540. "King Cotton" powered the state's economy prior to
the outbreak of the Civil War.

Remnants of Alabama's plantation days can still be seen in Mobile,
where an exquisite collection of antebellum architecture mingles with the
story of Admiral David Farragut and his Union victories. While some
still cling to the notion of the Old South and mint julep afternoons, Alabama has continued to stride toward the future as it reclaims its past.
Huntsville is a thriving center of the space industry, Birmingham has
evolved into a major cultural and medical center, and Montgomery, its
capital, is one of the South's most appealing destinations.

The literary stops in "Sweet Home Alabama" are enthralling and include a number of important writers and their landmarks. One of American literature's most enduring novels, *To Kill a Mockingbird*, attracts

thousands of visitors annually to Monroeville, the birthplace of Harper Lee. Truman Capote was a lifelong friend of Lee's; "A Christmas Memory" recalls his childhood in Alabama.

Winston Groom's *Forrest Gump* and Fannie Flagg's *Fried Green Tomatoes at the Whistlestop Café* are also products of the state. Tuscumbia is noteworthy as the birthplace of Helen Keller, and Montgomery provided the romantic setting for F. Scott and Zelda Fitzgerald's courtship.

⌐ Birmingham

> For lunch and supper you can have: fried chicken; pork chops and gravy; catfish; chicken and dumplings; or a barbecue plate; and your choice of three vegetables, biscuits or cornbread, and your drink and dessert—for 35¢.
>
> —FANNIE FLAGG,
> *Fried Green Tomatoes at the Whistle Stop Café*

ALABAMA'S LARGEST CITY is home to the **Irondale Café,** the inspiration for the setting of Fannie Flagg's beloved 1987 novel, *Fried Green Tomatoes at the Whistle Stop Café.* The eatery is located just east of Birmingham on I-20. You can still get such delectable southern fare as fried chicken and catfish, and of course the café's "world famous" fried green tomatoes, the most popular dish on the menu.

Flagg, a native of Birmingham, modeled the character of Idgie Threadgoode on her great-aunt Bess Fortenberry, who purchased the café located alongside the railroad tracks in 1932, during the Great Depression. A hangout for laborers working on the railroad and locals and travelers desiring a good, affordable southern meal, the place became a hit for its down-home cooking.

Flagg's novel was a long-running bestseller; a film adaptation released in 1991 starred Kathy Bates and Jessica Tandy. The author has become something of a celebrity at the café, and published a cookbook featuring some of its most-requested offerings.

The café has changed hands since Flagg wrote the novel but remains one of Birmingham's most popular stops. "Strangely enough," the author has said, "the first character in *Fried Green Tomatoes* was the café, and the town. I think a place can be as much a character in a novel as the people." One of the café's five dining rooms has a photographic exhibit on Flagg and her beloved book.

Irondale Café, 1906 1st Avenue North, Irondale, AL 35210 (205-956-5258; www.irondalecafe.com)

🅢 LITERARY LODGING

THE TUTWILER

Downtown Birmingham's Tutwiler dates back to 1913. Although the original fell to the wrecking ball in 1974, a completely restored Tutwiler opened at a different location in 2007 and has one of the splashiest restaurants in the city: the Century Restaurant. The towering property is managed by the Hilton Hotels & Resorts group as a Hampton Inn & Suites, but this is far from your ordinary chain hotel. The building is a National Historic Landmark of the railroad era, with décor inspired by the original hotel. A lovely lobby with marble floors, chandeliers, and brass banisters transports guests to another era. An exhibit of black-and-white photographs giving a brief history of the city is on display here as well.

The Tutwiler, 2021 Park Place, Birmingham, AL 35203 (205-322-2100; www.thetutwilerhotel.com)

⚙ EXCURSIONS AND DIVERSIONS

HISTORY AND CULTURE IN BIRMINGHAM

Civil rights history remains at the center of Birmingham's identity. The **Birmingham Civil Rights Institute** is a repository of information pertaining to the civil rights movement and the individuals involved with it, including Rosa Parks, Martin Luther King Jr., and the Freedom Riders. Artifacts on display include the door of the cell occupied by King when he wrote "Letter from a Birmingham Jail" in April 1963.

Yet there are a host of additional options to explore while visiting Alabama's largest city. For a cultural outing, the **Birmingham Museum of Art** holds one of the South's most esteemed American and African art collections, as well as one of the finest collections of Wedgwood china in the world. Docent-led tours focus on specific galleries within the museum. **Oscars,** its delightful dining spot, is ideal for Sunday brunch. The **McWane Science Center** has an IMAX theater as well as a variety of hands-on exhibits for children. The **Birmingham Botanical Gardens** are breathtaking in the spring when the flowers are in bloom. The Japanese Garden area is complete with a teahouse, making this stop unforgettable.

Birmingham Civil Rights Institute, 520 16th Street North, Birmingham, AL 35203 (205-328-9696; www.bcri.org)

Birmingham Museum of Art, 200 Rev. Abraham Woods, Jr. Boulevard, Birmingham, AL 35203 (205-254-2565; www.arts bma.org)

McWane Science Center, 200 19th Street North, Birmingham, AL 35203 (205-714-8300; www.mcwane.org)

Birmingham Botanical Gardens, 2612 Lane Park Road Birmingham, AL 35223 (205-414-3950; www.bbgardens.org)

ᐳ Monroeville

> *Maycomb was an old town, but it was a tired old town when I first knew it. In rainy weather the streets turned to red slop; grass grew on the sidewalks, the courthouse sagged in the square. . . . People moved slowly then. They ambled across the square, shuffled in and out of the stores around it, took their time about everything. A day was twenty-four hours long but seemed longer. There was no hurry, for there was nowhere to go, nothing to buy and no money to buy it with, nothing to see outside the boundaries of Maycomb County.*
>
> —HARPER LEE, *To Kill a Mockingbird*

THE POIGNANT STORY of Jem, Scout, Dill, Boo Radley, and Atticus Finch lives on at the **Monroe County Heritage Museum,** where exhibits showcase the literary achievement of Harper Lee, born in Monroeville in 1926. Lee's Pulitzer Prize–winning novel, *To Kill a Mockingbird*, centers on life in the fictional town of Maycomb, which was modeled on Monroeville during the Great Depression. Its depiction of family relationships and

growing up in the rural South—as well as coping with race relations—has made *To Kill a Mockingbird* both timely and classic.

More than 30,000 visitors travel to Monroeville annually, drawn by their interest in and affection for *To Kill a Mockingbird*. Designated the Literary Capital of Alabama, Monroeville is located between Mobile and Montgomery, and pays tribute to the novel seemingly around every corner. The **Monroe County Heritage Museum** takes as its subject Lee's novel, her connections to Monroeville, and her friendship with childhood chum Truman Capote.

The museum's *To Kill a Mockingbird* exhibit delves into Lee's early years in Monroeville, in her own words and through photographs. A 30-minute documentary film shows what the town must have been like during Lee's childhood.

The author, who in her later years has shunned publicity and rarely gives interviews, did open up about the

THE MONROE COUNTY HERITAGE MUSEUM

book in 1961 after winning the Pulitzer Prize. In one interview she said that the novel was "a love story pure and simple" about the South in general and Monroeville in particular. "The South," she said, "is still made up of thousands of tiny towns. There is a very definite social pattern in these towns that fascinates me."

In another interview granted in the 1960s she said of her novel: "It is and it isn't autobiographical. . . . What I did present as exactly as I could were the clime and tone, as I remember them, of the town in which I lived. From childhood on, I did sit in the courtroom watching my father argue cases and talk to juries." Lee's father, a lawyer, was the model for the central character in the book, and her admiration and love for him are evident in its pages. The Old Courthouse where he practiced is part of the museum. Set designers re-created this courtroom on a Hollywood soundstage for the 1962 film adaptation of *To Kill a Mockingbird*.

When Gregory Peck began to research his role as Atticus Finch, he met with Lee to discuss the character. They became lifelong friends, and when he was nominated for an Academy Award for his performance in the role, Lee gave him a gold pocket watch that belonged to her father as

a good-luck charm. He carried it with him the night he won the Oscar for Best Actor.

In April and May a theatrical performance of the book is performed by the **Mockingbird Players** in the amphitheater of the Monroe County Heritage Museum. The popular event is a major fund-raiser for the museum, now entering its 23rd year. But don't expect to see Lee at the performance; she lives quietly in Monroeville when visiting from New York and largely avoids any publicity associated with the book.

The friendship between Lee and Truman Capote has been well documented. The two grew up together in Monroeville, often playing together, much like her characters Scout and Dill. The Truman Capote exhibit at the Monroe County Heritage Museum chronicles his life in Monroeville through letters, photographs, and memorabilia. Capote's short story "A Christmas Memory" recalls his early experience in Monroeville.

Each spring Monroeville hosts the **Alabama Writers Symposium,** organized by the Alabama Center for Literary Arts at Monroeville's Alabama Southern Community College. The literary festival offers a weekend of readings, book signings by major authors, and discussions, with the main event being the presentation of the Harper Lee Award for Alabama's Distinguished Writer. Winston Groom, author of the 1986 novel *Forrest Gump,* is among the recipients of the prestigious annual award.

Monroe County Heritage Museum, 31 North Alabama Avenue, Monroeville, AL 36460 (251-575-7433; www.tokillamocking bird.com)

Alabama Writers Symposium (www.writerssymposium.org)

Montgomery

The sheath that held her soul has assumed significance—that was all.
She was a sun, radiant, growing, gathering light and storing it—then
after an eternity pouring it forth in a glance, the fragment of a sentence,
to that part of him that cherished all beauty and all illusion.
—F. SCOTT FITZGERALD, *The Beautiful and the Damned*

ON A WARM SUMMER'S EVENING in June 1918, one dashing lieutenant
by the name of F. Scott Fitzgerald met the love of his life. Zelda Sayre, a
Montgomery debutante, was attending a country-club dance when she cast
a glance at the charming midwesterner stationed at nearby Camp Sheridan.
His Irish good looks and her beguiling smile were the stuff of legends.
Thus began one of the most talked-about romances of the 20th century:
the "Scott and Zelda" story. In one letter to Scott, Zelda wrote, "Don't
you think I was made for you? I feel like you had me ordered—and I was
delivered to you—to be worn. I want you to wear me, like a watch-charm
or a button-hole bouquet—to the world."

Alabama's capital city provided the setting for the storied Fitzgerald
courtship and figures in *The Great Gatsby:* The novel's heroine, Daisy
Buchanan, is based largely on Zelda. Fitzgerald was stationed at Camp
Sheridan when he met the girl who would transform his life. Like
Gatsby—and in Fitzgerald's own words—"There was a "heightened sen-
sitivity" and gorgeousness about them, a "romantic readiness," as if the
sunlight that swirled around them would last forever.

Fitzgerald had arrived in Montgomery after a previous posting at
Camp Taylor in Louisville, Kentucky (see chapter 4 for Fitzgerald sites in
Louisville). It was a turning point in both his personal and professional
lives. If the East excited and enthralled him, finding its way into much of
his fiction, it was the South with its lulling tempo, faded dreams, and
courtly ways that appealed to his creative imagination.

Tracing Fitzgerald's steps in Montgomery begins at Union Station,
a Romanesque Revival structure dating back to 1898 that at one time wel-
comed over 40 passenger trains a day. Overlooking the banks of the Alabama River, this is where the budding writer arrived. Today the handsome
building, designated a National Historic Landmark, is an ideal starting
point for your Fitzgerald expedition.

Just a few blocks from Union Station—the present location of the Montgomery Visitors Center—is 6 Pleasant Avenue, the site of Zelda's now-demolished childhood home. Within easy reach of this area is Court Square Fountain on Dexter Avenue. Built in 1885, this is one of Montgomery's most historic landmarks and where Zelda often played as a child and went for walks in her later years.

The most significant Fitzgerald landmark is the **F. Scott and Zelda Fitzgerald Museum,** found at 919 Felder Avenue in the Cloverdale section of the city. This is the only museum devoted to the couple and the only one of their residences that can be toured. They rented the house in October 1931, following escapades in New York and Europe, to be near Zelda's family and to provide a more stable home environment for their only child, daughter Scottie, born in 1921. Their plan was to rent the house for six months then purchase property in Montgomery. When queried by the local newspaper about his feelings toward Montgomery, Fitzgerald replied, "You see, I'm not a stranger to Montgomery at all having been stationed here during the war and marrying a Montgomery girl, I have felt the warmth of the city's personality. . . . I'm going to like it here in Montgomery." But Fitzgerald's hopes were dashed when he was summoned back to Hollywood to earn money as a screenwriter to support their extravagant lifestyle. While living at the Felder residence he began serious work on *Tender Is the Night,* preferring to work on the back porch. Zelda also began work on a novel of her own, *Save Me the Waltz,* published in 1932.

With Scott away in California, Zelda's loneliness increased, adding to her deteriorating mental condition. When Fitzgerald returned from California for the Christmas holidays, he soon realized that a permanent residence in Montgomery was not going to work. In 1932 he took Zelda to Baltimore to the Johns Hopkins University Hospital. In due time he moved to Baltimore to begin another chapter in his life.

A tour through the Fitzgerald Museum offers an unparalleled perspective into the Fitzgeralds' stormy and tumultuous life. The downstairs rooms are the only ones open to the public. On view are family mementos, photographs, first editions, a fan he gave her, and a worn flapper headband that she made into a cigarette holder. Some of Zelda's paintings are also on display as well as worn family scrapbooks that showcase their fascinating and unsettled life. The house itself is marked with an Alabama Historic plaque describing the Fitzgerald connection.

⚭ Tuscumbia

*I believe that life is given us that we may grow in love, and I believe
that God is in me as the sun is in the color and fragrance of a flower—
the Light in my darkness, the Voice in my silence.*
—HELEN KELLER, *Light in My Darkness*

ROSES AND HONEYSUCKLE adorn **Ivy Green,** the cottage located in Alabama's Muscle Shoals area where Helen Keller was born in 1880. The house and grounds are open to the public as the **Helen Keller Birthplace.** The white clapboard cottage was built by her grandfather, and the well where Keller first learned the word *water* from her teacher Annie Sullivan is on the property.

Courtesy Library of Congress

Designated in 1954 as a shrine to Keller, the property is listed on the National Register of Historic Places. A 640-acre estate surrounds the cottage, which has been restored to reflect Keller's era and is filled with many personal mementos and family memorabilia. The house is a museum that chronicles Keller's life. Visitors can view the original Braille typewriter on which she typed her writings and correspondence. Keller was the author of 12 books, including her autobiography *The Story of My Life* (1903).

Touring the house gives visitors a renewed appreciation for this remarkable human being. Annually the **Helen Keller Festival** pays tribute to Keller with a performance of William Gibson's play *The Miracle Worker.* Parades, outdoor events, and readings are featured at this event, held the last week of June.

THE FAMOUS WELL

Ivy Green, 300 North Commons Street, West Tuscumbia, AL 35674 (256-383-4066; www.helenkellerbirthplace.org)

Helen Keller Festival (www.helenkellerfestival.com)

F. Scott and Zelda Fitzgerald Museum, 919 Felder Avenue, Montgomery, AL 36106 (334-264-4222; www.fitzgerald museum.net)

Montgomery Area Chamber of Commerce Convention & Visitor Bureau, Montgomery Union Station and Train Shed, 300 Water Street, Montgomery, AL 36104 (334-261-1100 or 1-800-240-9452; visitor center: 334-262-0013; www.visiting montgomery.com)

🍁 LITERARY LODGING

RED BLUFF COTTAGE

Located in Montgomery's historic Cottage Hill District, just minutes from the F. Scott and Zelda Fitzgerald Museum, the four-room Red Bluff Cottage is an intimate inn overlooking the Alabama River. The purpose-built B&B is in the style of a 19th-century Victorian raised cottage. Montgomery's skyline and the Alabama River are visible from the veranda. A full southern breakfast is included.

Red Bluff Cottage, 551 Clay Street, Montgomery, AL 36104 (334-264-0056; www.redbluffcottage.com)

⊛ EXCURSIONS AND DIVERSIONS

EXPLORING MONTGOMERY

The **Alabama Shakespeare Festival** is a professional regional theater with performances staged at the Carolyn Blount Theatre, located in the Wynton M. Blount Cultural Park, just outside Montgomery. The theater presents first-class productions year-round, ranging from works by Shakespeare to those of contemporary playwrights. The theater sits alongside the **Montgomery Museum of Fine Arts,** which features works by Winslow Homer and folk art as well as periodic exhibitions of Zelda Fitzgerald's paintings.

Alabama Shakespeare Festival, 1 Festival Drive, Montgomery, AL 36117 (334-271-5354; www.asf.net)

Montgomery Museum of Fine Arts, 1 Museum Drive, Montgomery, AL 36117 (334-240-4333; www.mmfa.org)

🍸 LITERARY LODGING

COLD WATER INN

The Cold Water's antebellum exterior and luxurious interior are evocative of the Old South. Offering 74 rooms and a complimentary breakfast, the inn is convenient to Ivy Green and the Alabama Music Hall of Fame (see "Excursions and Diversions"). Although it is a modern hotel, it exudes southern hospitality and graciousness.

Cold Water Inn, 712 Highway 72W , Tuscumbia, AL 35674 (256-383-6844; www.coldwater-inn.com)

⚙ EXCURSIONS AND DIVERSIONS

EXPLORING TUSCUMBIA'S MUSICAL HERITAGE

Tuscumbia is renowned for its musical heritage, and the **Alabama Music Hall of Fame** is the area's most visited and popular attraction. Opened in 1990, it includes 500 inductees, representing rock and roll, rhythm and blues, gospel, and country and western music.

The Muscle Shoals area has been called the Hit Recording Capital of the World because of the many popular songs that originated here. Another important musical attraction is the **W. C. Handy Home and Museum,** located in nearby Florence. The restored home of the father of the blues has some of his musical instruments on display as well as original sheet music.

THE HELLEN KELLER BIRTHPLACE

Alabama Music Hall of Fame, 617 US 72, Tuscumbia, AL 35674 (256-381-4417; www.ala mhof.org)

W. C. Handy Home and Museum, 620 West College Street, Florence, AL 35630 (256-760-6434)

$\mathscr{F}$LORIDA

W HISPERS OF EXOTIC TALES fill many of Florida's literary
notebooks. It was a sense of adventure that lured so many
renowned literary talents to this frontier Eden. Florida pan-
thers once roamed the primitive landscape, where hammocks scrublands,
grassy swamps, and white-sand beaches outline a diverse landscape.

Florida's history is as rich as its flora and fauna. Seminole Indians
first settled the forested landscape. In 1513 Spanish explorer Juan Ponce
de León landed in what is today St. Augustine, the oldest European set-
tlement in the United States. But it was the runaway ambition of railroad
baron Henry Flagler in the 19th century that dramatically transformed
Florida into a vacation paradise.

Aquamarine waters, balmy winters, golden sunsets, and a string of
grand hotels continue to attract travelers to the state. All of the literary
names associated with Florida came here searching for something—for
Ernest Hemingway it was a place to write; for Stephen Crane, a point of
departure in his career as a war correspondent. Zane Grey wanted to fish
Florida's many waterways, while Marjorie Kinnan Rawlings discovered her
literary destiny here. To Zora Neale Hurston, Florida was where she experienced a reawakening of her literary voice. Other names on the Florida
literary tour should include Laura Riding Jackson, Walter Farley, Robert

Frost, Wallace Stevens, Elizabeth Bishop, and Tennessee Williams, all of whom fell under the state's spell.

From Key West to Miami and all along its Atlantic and Gulf Coasts, Florida offers travelers a wealth of literary sites associated with some of the country's most important poets, playwrights, and novelists.

ᐁ Captiva Island

> *Here on this island I have had space. Paradoxically, in this limited area, space has been forced upon me. . . . Here there is time; time to be quiet; time to work without pressure; time to think; time to watch the heron, watching with frozen patience for his prey. Time to look at the stars or to study a shell.*
>
> —ANNE MORROW LINDBERGH, *Gift from the Sea*

CERTAINLY ONE OF THE LOVELIEST and most unspoiled areas of Florida is Captiva Island. Miles away from the endless theme parks of Orlando and Miami's bright lights, this is where Anne Morrow Lindbergh escaped with her famous aviator husband, Charles Lindbergh, in the 1930s and '40s. The island paradise off Florida's west coast became an idyllic retreat for the author, who spent considerable time on the island near the **'Tween Waters Inn** (see "Literary Lodging") during her many visits. It is where she wrote her most famous book, *Gift from the Sea,* published in 1955 and an international bestseller.

The barrier island awash with seashells is known for its winding pathways, abundant bird life, and serenity. The Lindberghs sought privacy here, usually renting a small cottage on Captiva that became their hideaway, enabling them to escape the glaring lights of the media. **The Bailey-Matthews Shell Museum,** on nearby Sanibel Island, exhibits the native shells that so captivated Lindbergh.

The Bailey-Matthews Shell Museum, 3075 Sanibel-Captiva Road, Sanibel, FL 33957 (239-395-2233; www.shellmuseum .org)

§ LITERARY LODGING

'TWEEN WATERS INN

Nestled amid the pines between the Gulf of Mexico and Pine Island Sound are 13 acres home to the 'Tween Waters Inn. Guests started arriving at this enchanting locale beginning in the early 1930s. Today several of the 19 historic cottages are named after famous guests; there is both an Anne Morrow Lindbergh Cottage and a Charles Lindbergh Cottage. In addition to the Lindberghs, Teddy Roosevelt visited this site to go deep-sea fishing. It is also where famed cartoonist J. "Ding" Darling, whom the nearby refuge is named after, visited. Listed on the National Register of Historic Places in 2011, the inn with its **Old Captiva House** restaurant, first built as a one-room schoolhouse, has attracted writers, artists, and explorers over the years. A history gallery in the restaurant details the inn's early days, highlighting some of its more illustrious guests.

'Tween Waters Inn Island Resort, 15951 Captiva Drive, Captiva, FL 33924 (1-800-223-5865; www.tween-waters.com)

® EXCURSIONS AND DIVERSIONS

CABBAGE KEY

> *Every crucial experience can be regarded as a setback—or the start of a new kind of development.*
>
> —MARY ROBERTS RINEHART

Accessible from Captiva Island, Cabbage Key offers a taste of Old Florida. The laid-back atmosphere immortalized by native Floridian singer and songwriter Jimmy Buffett can be enjoyed at this island getaway. Cabbage Key is situated at Channel Marker 60. Bottlenose dolphins may escort you as you make your way by boat—the only way to reach the island outpost.

"Mañanaville" best describes this little corner of Florida where mystery writer Mary Roberts Rinehart, of "The butler did it" fame, came beginning in the 1930s, both for health reasons and to work on her mystery novels. Rinehart's former island residence is now the **Cabbage Key Inn and Restaurant.** The eatery is known for the thousands of dollar bills covering the walls; feel free to add one of your own. Jimmy Buffett wrote "Cheeseburger in Paradise" after a visit here. The popular watering hole is often crowded during the high season, with the fall and early spring sublime times to visit this secluded hideaway.

Literary travelers considering an overnight here have a good option in the **Rinehart Cottage.** Constructed in the early 1930s, this cozy Cabbage Key abode was originally home to the caretaker for the Rinehart family. It's now a vacation rental, and includes two bedrooms, one bathroom, a living room, and a screened-in front porch that overlooks the marina. For information, contact Cabbage Key, Inc.

Cabbage Key Cruise, Captiva Cruises (239-472-5300; captiva cruises.com)

Cabbage Key Inn and Restaurant, Cabbage Key, Inc., PO Box 200, Pineland, FL 33945 (239-283-2278; www.cabbagekey .com)

✿ EXCURSIONS AND DIVERSIONS

THE LEE ISLAND COAST

Beautiful beaches, bountiful birding hot spots, and an array of outdoor pleasures await you on Florida's Lee Island Coast. Stretching from Fort Myers Beach to Sanibel and Captiva Islands, this region of Florida is located in the state's southwest corner. It's a naturalist's dream: miles upon miles of unspoiled wilderness landscapes, little touched since Anne Morrow Lindbergh and Mary Roberts Rinehart looked out on them.

From Audubon's **Corkscrew Swamp Sanctuary** to the **J. N. "Ding" Darling Refuge,** this area is ideal for travelers interested in not only seeking literary sites but also exploring some of the state's most renowned natural areas. Most of these form a sort of necklace around Fort Myers; more than 1 million acres of nature sanctuaries dot the landscape. Included among them are the **Sanibel-Captiva Conservation Foundation, Calusa Nature Center, Carl E. Johnson State Park at Lovers Key, Matanzas Pass Wilderness Preserve, Six-Mile Cypress Slough Preserve,** and Corkscrew Swamp Sanctuary.

Along with this abundance of natural areas, Fort Myers is

endowed with a variety of cultural sites. The **Thomas Edison and Henry Ford Winter Estates** afford a rare opportunity for learning more about two of America's most eminent inventors. Edison and Ford, best friends, lived next door in Fort Myers. Edison was the first to settle in the area. A giant banyan tree greets visitors to his 14-acre property, awash with lush gardens and sweeping views of the river. Named Seminole Lodge by Edison, who also designed the house, the main structure was constructed in Fairfield, Maine, and shipped in parts to Florida aboard four sailing schooners. The visitors center is where you begin your guided tour. Edison, who lived here from 1886 until his death in 1931, perfected many of his inventions while in residence, including the incandescent lightbulb, the motion-picture camera, and the phonograph.

The Henry Ford Home is on a much smaller scale but every bit as interesting. The auto magnate purchased the house in 1916 to escape the harsh Michigan winters and to be near his lifelong friend. The highlight of the tour is the garage, with its assortment of antique Fords.

Audubon Corkscrew Swamp Sanctuary, 375 Sanctuary Road West, Naples, FL 34120 (239-348-9151; wwwcorkscrew swamp.org)

J. N. "Ding" Darling Refuge, 1 Wildlife Drive, Sanibel, FL 33957 (239-472-1100; www.fws.gov/dingdarling)

Sanibel-Captiva Conservation Foundation, 3333 Sanibel-Captiva Road, Sanibel, FL 33957 (239-472-2329; www.sccf.org)

Calusa Nature Center, 3450 Ortiz Avenue, Fort Myers, FL 33905 (239-275-3435; www.calusanature.org)

Carl E. Johnson State Park at Lovers Key, 8700 Estero Boulevard, Fort Myers Beach, FL 33931 (239-463-4588; www.floridastateparks.org/loverskey)

Matanzas Pass Wilderness Preserve, 303 & 307 Nature View Court, Fort Myers Beach, FL 33931 (www.leeparks.org)

Six-Mile Cypress Slough Preserve, 7791 Penzance Boulevard, Fort Myers, FL 33966 (239-533-7550; www.leeparks.org /sixmile)

Edison & Ford Winter Estates, 2350 McGregor Boulevard, Fort Myers, FL (239-334-7419; www.edisonfordwinterestates.org)

∽ Cross Creek

> *Cross Creek belongs to the wind and the rain, to the sun and the seasons, to the cosmic secrecy of seed, and beyond all, to time.*
> —MARJORIE KINNAN RAWLINGS, *Cross Creek*

MARJORIE KINNAN RAWLINGS'S GRAVE SITE is at Antioch Cemetery in Island Grove, located just a few miles from her Cross Creek home. Rawlings settled here in 1928 to cultivate an orange grove, and to write. Deep in the heart of Florida's Alachua County—near Gainesville and on the fringes of Ocala National Forest—Cross Creek is a naturalist's dream where deer, wild turkeys, pileated woodpeckers, alligators, and river otters live in abundance. The remote and primitive setting unleashed Rawlings's creative spirit.

"When I came to the Creek," she wrote in her memoir *Cross Creek,* "I knew the old grove and the farmhouse at once as home." The simple cracker-style farmhouse, with its tilted roof and open porches, is surrounded by a dense forest of palmettos and scrubland. Its peaceful atmosphere influenced her most famous work, *The Yearling,* for which she was awarded the Pulitzer Prize in 1939.

The veranda on the front porch is where she did most of her writing, usually in the early mornings. The farmhouse, as she describes it in *Cross Creek,* "sat snugly then as now under tall old orange trees, and had a simple grace of line, low, rambling and one-storied."

The farmhouse consists of three separate structures connected by a bathroom, open verandas, and screen porches. The eight-room house is typical of the "Old Florida" design of the 1920s and early '30s. It is flanked by a barn and vegetable garden, where bald eagles, deer, and sandhill cranes can be seen roaming about.

Rawlings cultivated a garden and cooked many of her own meals in the stark kitchen, including alligator stew. In *Cross Creek* she elaborates on her fondness for the area as a world unto itself: "Cross Creek is a bend in a country road, by land, and the flowing of Lochloosa Lake into Orange

Lake, by water. We are four miles west of the small village of Orange Grove, nine miles east of a turpentine still, and on the other side we do not count distance at all, for the two lakes and the broad marshes create an infinite space between us and the horizon."

The guest bedroom is where her editor Maxwell Perkins stayed during a trip to Key West to visit Hemingway. In fact, it was Perkins who discovered Rawlings after reading the many stories she contributed to *Scribner's Magazine*. Recognizing her innate love of the land, he persuaded her to write a novel about the landscape she loved so dearly, and that is how the story of *The Yearling* began. Zora Neale Hurston also visited her at the property, as did close friend Margaret Mitchell.

"Enchantment," she wrote, "lies in different things for each of us. For me, it is in this: to step out of the bright sunlight into the shade of orange trees; to walk under the arched canopy of their jadelike leaves; to see the long aisles of lichened trunks stretch ahead in a geometric rhythm; to feel the mystery of a seclusion that yet has shafts of light striking through it. This is the essence of an ancient and secret magic."

Rawlings eventually left Cross Creek for St. Augustine, where she lived until her death in 1953. She bequeathed the Cross Creek house and most of its belongings to the University of Florida. The house and grounds are maintained and managed by Florida State Parks; the homestead is located approximately 4 miles west of Island Grove off US 301.

Marjorie Kinnan Rawlings Historic State Park, 18700 South County Road 325, Cross Creek, FL 32640 (352-466-3672; www.floridastateparks.org/marjoriekinnanrawlings)

⊛ EXCURSIONS AND DIVERSIONS

THE FLORIDA OF MARJORIE KINNAN RAWLINGS

Literary travelers can immerse themselves in the natural landscape that so inspired Marjorie Kinnan Rawlings by visiting **Ocala National Forest**—the second largest national forest in the United States.

Encompassing more than 607 square miles, this frontier wilderness of longleaf pines and scrubland is home to Florida's largest population of black bears; it is a haven as well for bobcats, river otters, red and gray foxes, and white-tailed deer. The forest has an abundance of water resources: some 600 lakes and rivers, and several natural springs where visitors can swim, snorkel, and dive year-round.

Surrounded by live oaks, **Juniper Springs** is one of the forest's most dazzling areas, and a prime spot for bird-watching. **Lake George** and **Lake Kerr** are top locations for bass fishing. Ocala National Forest also has 100 miles of designated trails for hiking and horseback riding, and a mountain bike trail that connects **Clearwater Lake Recreation Area** to the **Alexander Springs Recreation Area.**

The **Florida Black Bear Scenic Byway** travels through 60 miles of the forest if you prefer to experience its beauty from the comfort of your car. Three visitors centers within the park recommend sites and areas for outdoor activities, camping, and recreational facilities.

Ocala National Forest, Marion, FL (352-236-0288; www.fs .usda.gov/ocala)

ᴥ Daytona Beach

The Commodore was cleared with a cargo of arms and munitions for Cuba. There was none of that extreme modesty about the proceeding which had marked previous departures of the famous tug. She loaded up as placidly as if she were going to carry oranges to New York, instead of Remingtons to Cuba.

—Stephen Crane

THE BRIGHT BEACON LIGHT of **Ponce Inlet Lighthouse,** formerly known as the Mosquito Inlet Lighthouse, saved Stephen Crane's life.

It was on a New Year's Eve afternoon in 1896 that the daring 25-year-old Crane, author of the Civil War novel *The Red Badge of Courage,* boarded the steamer tug SS *Commodore* in Jacksonville. She was bound for Cuba loaded with ammunition, rifles, and a crew of more than twenty-five. Crane had signed on as a seaman so he could report on the insurrection against Spain for a New York syndicate. Paid $700 in gold, the journalist was unaware that just a few hours later the ship would be threatened with heavy seas and a shipwreck.

As the *Commodore* made her way down the St. John's River in heavy fog, she hit a sandbar, damaging the hull and causing a leak in the boiler room, eventually bringing the vessel to a virtual standstill. With the weather rapidly deteriorating, the crew was forced to abandon the disabled ship.

"As darkness came upon the waters," Crane wrote, "the *Commodore's* wake was a broad, flaming path of blue and silver phosphorescence, and as her stout bow lunged at the great black waves she threw flashing, roaring cascades to either side."

Crane, along with the *Commodore's* captain Murphy, oiler William Higgins, and shipmate Steward Montgomery, sized up their perilous situation and climbed into a 10-foot lifeboat to reach safety. (We do not know for sure how many of the other crew members were lost at sea.) Stranded for over 30 hours at sea, Murphy issued a distress call to no avail. On January 3, just days after embarking from Jacksonville, the men decided to swim to shore, lit by the bright beacon of the Mosquito Inlet Lighthouse.

STEPHEN CRANE, c. 1899
Wikimedia Commons, p.d.

Close to drowning, Crane and his companions were finally assisted by someone onshore. "John Kitchell of Daytona," wrote Crane in his newspaper account of the rescue, "came running down the beach, and as he ran the air was filled with clothes. If he had pulled a single lever and undressed, even as the fire horses harness, he could not to me seem to have stripped with more speed. He dashed into the water and grabbed the cook. Then he went after the captain, but the captain sent him to me, and then it was that we saw Billy Higgins lying with his forehead on sand that was clear of the water, and he was dead."

The terrifying ordeal was the inspiration for Crane's "The Open Boat," a short story written some months after the shipwreck and published in *Scribner's Magazine*. Praised by close friend and contemporary H. G. Wells, the story described the harrowing event in detail. "None of them," Crane wrote of the lifeboat's occupants, "knew the color of the sky. Their eyes glanced level, and were fastened upon the waves that swept toward them. These waves were of the hue of slate, save for the tops, which were of foaming white, and all of the men knew the colors of the sea. The horizon narrowed and widened, and dipped and rose, and at all times its edge was jagged with waves that seemed thrust up in points like rocks."

Captain Murphy also applauded Crane's bravery in an interview with the *New York Post.* "That man Crane is the spunkiest fellow out. . . . Crane was the first man to stagger to the beach looking for houses. He's a thoroughbred and a brave man too with plenty of grit."

Divers set out in the early 1980s to find the remains of the SS *Commodore.* Artifacts from the ship were discovered 12 miles off Daytona's coast and are now on display at the **Ponce de Leon Inlet Lighthouse and Museum.** Remington rifles were among the items recovered from the ship's last voyage.

Another significant Crane connection is found at **Lilian Place,** formerly a bed & breakfast and presently part of the Heritage Preservation Trust of Volusia County. The house has documents showing that Crane stayed in the house following the shipwreck and before heading back to Jacksonville. The Italianate High Victorian building is one of Daytona's oldest structures and at this writing under reconstruction; once the restoration is complete there will be a small exhibit devoted to Crane. From Lilian Place, Crane headed back to Jacksonville, where he wrote "The Open Boat." He died several years later of tuberculosis, at the age of 28.

Ponce de Leon Inlet Lighthouse and Museum, 4931 South Peninsula Drive, Ponce Inlet, FL 32127 (386-761-1821; www.ponceinlet.org)

Lilian Place Historical Home, 111 Silver Beach Avenue, Daytona Beach, FL 32118 (386-299-4974; www.lilianplace.org)

᥌ Eatonville

*So I rounded Park Lake and came speeding down the straight stretch
into Eatonville, the city of five lakes, three croquet courts, three hundred
brown skins, three hundred good swimmers, plenty guavas, two schools,
and no jail-house.*

—ZORA NEALE HURSTON, *Mules and Men*

A VOICE OF THE HARLEM RENAISSANCE, Zora Neale Hurston grew
up in Eatonville, a small rural community 10 miles northeast of Orlando.
The oldest African-American-chartered municipality in the United States,
Eatonville was a strong influence on Hurston's development as a novelist,
folklorist, and anthropologist. Born in 1891, Hurston entered Howard
University in 1918 and went on to study at Barnard, where she earned a
BA in anthropology in 1927.

In the introduction to her influential collection of African American
folktales, *Mules and Men*, published in 1935, Hurston wrote, "I was glad
when somebody told me, 'You may go and collect Negro folklore.' In a
way it would not be a new experience for me. . . . It was only when I was
off in college, away from my native surroundings, that I could see myself
like somebody else and stand off and look at my garments."

Hurston is best known for her autobiography, *Dust Tracks on a Road,*
published in 1942, and the 1937 novel *Their Eyes Were Watching God.* She co-
wrote *Mule Bone: A Comedy of Negro Life in Three Acts* with Langston Hughes.
It was published posthumously in 1991.

Hughes said of his close friend and contemporary, "She was full of
sidesplitting anecdotes, humorous tales, and tragicomic stories, remembered out of her life in the South as a daughter of a traveling minister of
God. She could make you laugh one minute and cry the next."

Today Hurston's legacy is honored at the **Zora Neale Hurston Festival of the Arts and Humanities,** presented annually by the Association
to Preserve the Eatonville Community (PEC). Initiated in 1990, the event
celebrates her life through artistic competitions, educational presentations,
and street festivals highlighting African American culture. Her name graces
the **Zora Neale Hurston National Museum of Fine Arts,** also sponsored
by PEC. The Hurston, as it is familiarly known, showcases the works of
artists of African descent.

During her life Hurston struggled to support herself as a writer, and fame eluded her. "There is no great sorrow dammed up in my soul, nor lurking behind my eyes," she wrote of her circumstances. "I do not mind at all. . . . I do not weep at the world—I am too busy sharpening my oyster knife."

After settling in Fort Pierce, Florida, in her later years and working as a teacher, she suffered a stroke in 1959 and died at the St. Lucie County Welfare Home on January 28, 1960. She was buried in an unmarked grave in the **Garden of Heavenly Rest Cemetery,** in Fort Pierce. Although her works languished in obscurity for several decades, the 1970s saw renewed interest in Hurston's writings, and today she is considered an important figure in American literature. In 1973 novelist Alice Walker, author of *The Color Purple,* placed a headstone on her grave inscribed, "A Genius of the South 1901–1960, Novelist, Folklorist, Anthropologist."

Zora Neale Hurston Festival of the Arts and Humanities, Eatonville, FL 32751 (407-647-3307; zorafestival.org)

Zora Neale Hurston National Museum of Fine Arts, 227 East Kennedy Boulevard, Eatonville, FL 32751 (407-647-3307; www.zoranealehurstonmuseum.com)

ᥱ Long Key

Fishing keeps men boys longer than any other pursuit!

—ZANE GREY

DEPARTING MIAMI and traveling the Overseas Highway en route to Key West, travelers are surrounded by shimmering waters on either side. Brown pelicans, great blue herons, and magnificent frigate birds accompany the drive through a series of small islands and villages from Key Largo to Islamorada, Long Key, and Key West, which lies at Florida's southernmost tip.

Each of these destinations displays its own brand of beauty. Long Key, approximately one hour from Key West, particularly captivated Zane Grey. It was here between 1910 and 1922 that the Ohio-born writer—best known for western adventure stories, including *Riders of the Purple Sage*—

often came to fish and write. The idyllic sportsman's paradise provided both the perfect backdrop for his passion for fishing and a serene setting to write. Grey bunked down in Hammerhead Cottage at the Long Key Fishing Camp—one of Henry Flagler's many creations catering to the wealthy and adventurous who desired to fish "big waters for the big fish."

In his book *The Bonefish Brigade*, Grey elaborated on his search for the big one. "I was sinking into what may be termed bonefish oblivion—a combination of suspense, dream, and sleep—when I had a tremendous strike. It sort of paralyzed me. . . . Sharp and hard I came up on a live weight. There was a quivering of my tight line. My rod bent double. The old thrill went over me, deep and wonderful sensation. Then the shallow water opened with a sudden thump and mud colored the spray. I had hooked a heavy bonefish."

Grey, who had been trained as a dentist and practiced in New York City, adored Long Key, Duck Key, and Grassy Key, where he'd write early in the morning and then head out for an all-day fishing trip. When he returned in the evening he would feast on stone crabs and key lime pie and finish his day editing the morning's work. He wrote to fish and fished to write; these were his two most ardent passions. When Flagler's Florida East Coast Railway was completed, Grey had been one of the first to travel on the modern marvel that connected Miami to the Keys. It provided him with serene surroundings far removed from the demands of Hollywood and the next big western being adapted for the screen from one of his books. Long Key is where he completed *Wild Horse Mesa* and *Code of the West*.

In 1935 when a violent hurricane devastated much of Flagler's rail line and the Long Key Fishing Camp, Grey lamented the end of an era. "It is sad," he wrote, "to think that Long Key, doomed by a hurricane, is gone forever. But the memory of that long white winding lonely shore of coral sand, and the green reef, and the blue Gulf Stream will live in memory. . . ."

Grey's fishing passion is celebrated at the **Zane Grey Long Key Lounge,** on the second floor of the Bass Pro Shops' Worldwide Sportsman in Islamorada. An original oil painting over the antique fireplace is a color reproduction of a photo commemorating the largest marlin taken on a rod and reel by Grey. Other artifacts on display purchased from the Zane Grey Foundation include a cabinet and other items from Grey's dental practice, photographs, rods and reels, and books. Visitors can also enjoy cocktails and menu offerings including stone crabs here.

Zane Grey Long Key Lounge, 81576 Overseas Highway, Islamorada, FL 33036 (mile marker 81.5, located in the Bass Pro Shops; 305-664-5071; http://restaurants.basspro.com/Zane GreyLounge/OurStory.aspx)

🐚 LITERARY LODGING

CHEECA LODGE & SPA

If Zane Grey were looking for accommodations while he fished Florida's waters today, he would most likely opt for this ultra-luxurious resort. The Cheeca Lodge & Spa in Islamorada—midway between Miami and Key West—dates back to 1946 and recalls a tropical estate nestled amid lush gardens, cascading waterfalls, and sparkling swimming pools. A West Indies motif makes the lodge a favorite of both avid anglers and discerning travelers.

Known as the sport fishing capital of the world, Islamorada is an angler's paradise. Sport fishermen from around the globe travel to Cheeca Lodge to enjoy first-class accommodations and a multitude of outdoor activities, including sea kayaking, bicycling, golf, and tennis. Anglers can charter a boat or fish off a 525-foot pier jutting out in the azure-blue Atlantic. The resort has an 1,100-foot palm-lined beach and a saltwater lagoon stocked with native fish. Spa treatments and a variety of dining options round out the experience.

Among the lodge's first guests were President Harry Truman and newsman Edward R. Murrow. More recently, President George H. W. Bush frequented the resort to enjoy his favorite pastime. Bush co-founded the George Bush Cheeca Lodge Bonefish Tournament in 1994, and in 2002 the lodge officially named its most luxurious accommodations after the former president.

Cheeca Lodge & Spa, 81801 Overseas Highway (mile marker 82), Islamorada, FL 33036 (305-664-4651; www.cheeca.com)

Key West

We have a fine house here and the kids are all well. Also four coons, a possum, 18 goldfish, three peacocks and a yard with fig tree, lime tree. Very fine the way Pauline has fixed it. We have been (and are) damned happy.

—ERNEST HEMINGWAY,
LETTER TO JANET FLANNER, KEY WEST, APRIL 8, 1933

ERNEST HEMINGWAY'S STUDIO
Courtesy of the Hemingway House & Museum

A BRILLIANT BLUE SKY guides you from Long Key to Key West—a destination that has attracted a host of writers but none more important than Ernest Hemingway. Like Zane Grey before him, Hemingway found Florida an ideal locale to pursue his two most ardent passions: fishing and writing. Key West's gingerbread architecture, caressing breezes, and blazing sunsets beckoned the author who gave us *A Farewell to Arms, The Snows of Kilimanjaro, The Old Man and the Sea,* and *To Have and Have Not.*

Waiting for the arrival of a Ford Roadster is what initially lured the writer to Key West—but it was also on the advice of literary friend John Dos Passos that Hemingway decided to visit and eventually settle in the area. Hemingway and his second wife, Pauline, traveled to Key West to pick up the Ford in 1929, but when it was delayed the dealership offered the couple a second-floor apartment above the showroom at 314 Simonton Street. It was during this period that he began serious work on *A Farewell to Arms.* Following several visits, they decided to purchase a home in 1931 at 907 Whitehead Street. Settling in the area marked a major turning point in the author's life.

The limestone Spanish colonial two-story house built in 1851 by marine architect Asa Tift became Hemingway's writing hideaway until 1940. It is where he completed a major portion of his most important writing.

Walking the rooms, you can view an array of Hemingway's personal belongings—hunting trophies from Africa, a ceramic cat that was a gift from Spanish painter Pablo Picasso, a white figurine that was given to him by actress Marlene Dietrich. There is also a figurine of a bullfighter as well as a chair used on the set of *The Fifth Column.* The Whitehead home became a gathering place for a host of A-list writers and editors, including Archibald MacLeish, Sinclair Lewis, Thornton Wilder, and Hemingway's editor, Maxwell Perkins.

The house is also home to a legion of six-toed cats, many of whom might be direct descendants of Hemingway's cats. If you stroll around the swimming pool—one of the first built in Key West, at a cost of $20,000—you will probably spot one of these famous felines.

To the literary traveler, the carriage house behind the main house is the main draw. This is the writer's inner sanctum, where Hemingway the writer went to work every day. Usually in the morning, he wrote his first drafts in longhand prior to tapping them out on his Royal typewriter. A selection of his most personal possessions is on display in the cottage, including photographs, books, and more. Light and airy, this room evokes a literary ambience.

In an interview many years later with his friend A. E. Hotchner, author of *Papa Hemingway: Personal Memoir,* Hemingway reflected on his writing life in the studio. "This is where I wrote 'The Snows of Kilimanjaro,' upstairs here, and that's as good as I've any right to be," he said, adding that "by the time I finished 'The Snows of Kilimanjaro,' I had put into it the material for four novels, distilled and compressed, nothing held back because I had declared to win with it. It took me a long time to write another story after that because I knew I could never write another as good as 'Kilimanjaro.' Don't think I ever did." In Key West, Hemingway affirmed, "Old as I am, I continue to be amazed at the sudden emergence of daffodils and stories."

If his mornings were devoted to writing, his afternoons were spent fishing aboard his boat, the *Pilar,* with friends Charlie Thompson and Joe Russell. Hemingway owned the Key West home until his death in 1961. His sons decided to sell the house and its contents to Bernice Dickson, a local businesswoman who turned it into a museum in 1964. Four years later it was designated a National Historic Landmark. It is now one of the nation's most visited literary sites, and among Key West's most treasured landmarks.

Key West has a host of Hemingway sites. **Sloppy Joes** at 201 Duval Street is another must-see establishment. Although the original saloon that Hemingway frequented was located at 428 Green Street, Sloppy Joes continues to wax the Hemingway myth. Annually this colorful saloon hosts the Hemingway Days Festival, which includes a short-story competition, readings, a look-alike contest, and other events celebrating Hemingway's Key West connections.

Another possible stop for travelers is the **Basilica of St. Mary Star of the Sea.** Dating to 1904, this is where one of Hemingway's sons, Gregory, was baptized.

> **Ernest Hemingway Home and Museum,** 907 Whitehead Street, Key West, FL 33040 (305-294-1136; www.hemingwayhome .com)
>
> **Sloppy Joe's,** 201 Duval Street, Key West FL 33040 (305-294-5717; www.sloppyjoes.com)
>
> **Cap't. Tony's Saloon,** 428 Greene Street, Key West, FL 33040 (305-294-1838; www.capttonyssaloon.com)
>
> **Hemingway Days** (www.hemingwaydays.org)
>
> **Basilica of St. Mary Star of the Sea,** 1010 Windsor Lane, Key West, FL 33040 (305-294-1018; www.keywestcatholicparish .org)

✿ EXCURSIONS AND DIVERSIONS

OUTINGS AROUND KEY WEST

One of the most spectacular outings you can take in the spirit of Papa Hemingway is a boat cruise out to the **Dry Tortugas National Park.** Located some 70 miles west of Key West in the Gulf of Mexico, this is where the writer felt most at home on his many fishing trips. The park is accessible only by boat or seaplane.

Activities abound at this sea destination, including camping, fishing, bird-watching, and some of the best snorkeling in the world. For birding enthusiasts the area is incomparable; you can usually see the magnificent frigate bird, peregrine falcons, and an array of shorebirds. You might also spot sea turtles.

Some other recommended outings while in the area should include **Truman's Little White House,** which was originally a naval station during the Spanish American War. Later, President Harry S. Truman used it as his winter White House. The **John James Audubon House & Tropical Gardens** are found a few doors down from the Hemingway home on Whitehead Street. This is where the famed naturalist and painter sketched and painted many of the works in his "Birds of America" series. The tiny cottage has been restored to depict Audubon's era.

Dry Tortugas National Park, PO Box 6208, Key West, FL 33041 (305-242-7700; www.nps.gov)

Dry Tortugas National Park Ferry, *Yankee Freedom III,* 240 Margaret Street, Key West, FL 33040 (1-800-634-0939; www.yankeefreedom.com)

Truman Little White House, 111 Front Street, Key West, FL (305-294-9911; www.trumanlittlewhitehouse.com)

John James Audubon House & Tropical Gardens, 205 White-head Street, Key West, FL 33040 (305-294-2116 or 1-877-294-2470; www.audubonhouse.com)

TENNESSEE WILLIAMS AND THE "MAD HOUSE"

Tennessee Williams's name is not far behind that of Hemingway on a Key West literary tour. The Mississippi-born playwright first discovered the island paradise in 1941—just 10 years after Hemingway put down roots at his Whitehead Street address. Key West's eternal sunshine and "mañana" attitude appealed to the writer, who first visited with his grandfather Walter Dakin. He admitted in an interview that he liked the area because "I love swimming. It was January, and I had to go someplace where I could swim in the winter so I came down here because it was the southernmost point, and I was immediately enchanted by the place. It was so much more primitive in those early days."

Following several visits from New Orleans and New York, Williams purchased a home in 1949 at 1431 Duncan Street. This secluded hideaway is awash in greenery and has a pool and writing studio that he called the Mad House. While residing in the bunga-low, he swam, wrote, and entertained close friends Truman Capote,

Carson McCullers, and Gore Vidal. He completed *Summer and Smoke* in Key West in 1946 and later *The Night of the Iguana*.

The home is now privately owned, but a plaque donated by the Friends of Libraries USA reads, "Residence of playwright Tennessee Williams," and includes the famous quote from *A Streetcar Named Desire*, "I have always depended on the kindness of strangers." The theater at Florida Keys Community College—Key West's premier cultural venue—is named after Williams.

POETS IN KEY WEST

In the 20th century a number of American poets traveled to Key West for its natural beauty. It became a haven for writers, poets, and artists, who found its relaxing atmosphere and warm winters an ideal setting for creative endeavors. Hemingway and Williams were not alone in finding creative inspiration in Key West. Poets Elizabeth Bishop and Robert Frost had residences in town, and Wallace Stevens enjoyed the comforts at the Casa Marina Hotel (see "Literary Lodging").

On Bishop's first visit to the island, she rented a small apartment at 529 Whitehead Street. From 1938 until 1946 she resided in a 19th-century yellow clapboard eyebrow house located at 624 White Street. A historical plaque dedicated in 1993 by the Friends of Libraries USA commemorates Bishop's time there. The White Street residence is where Bishop completed her first book of verse, *North and South,* published in 1946. Today the home is privately owned and off limits for touring. Not far from Bishop's former address, on the grounds of 410 Carolina Street, is the tiny cottage that Robert Frost lived in intermittently as a guest from 1941 until 1960. Here Frost entertained many literary visitors, including Wallace Stevens and Archibald MacLeish. A plaque dedicated in 1995 by the Friends of Libraries honors the poet. The cottage is now privately owned.

LITERARY LODGING

THE CASA MARINA

Referred to as the House by the Sea, the Casa Marina was built by Henry Flagler; it opened its doors to great fanfare on New Year's

Eve 1920. The AAA Four-Diamond establishment—managed under the Hilton's Waldorf Astoria banner—is located within easy reach of the Hemingway Home and other literary sites. It offers 1,100 feet of private beach, making it one of the most desirable lodging spots in Key West. Henry Flagler's luxurious touches are found throughout, from the terrace doors to the hardwood floors and Spanish Mediterranean architecture.

The hotel ushered in the glamorous Roaring Twenties, attracting Hollywood royalty, Presidents Warren G. Harding and Harry Truman, as well as writers Ernest Hemingway and Wallace Stevens. Hemingway usually came attired in sandals and shorts for lunch; Stevens was more apt to dress for dinner. Stevens enjoyed 18 winters at the hotel, from 1922 until 1940, staying for two to three weeks. On his first encounter with the area he remarked, "It was very much like a cloud full of Cuban senoritas, coconut palms, and waiters carrying ice water." Today the hotel remembers its most regular literary visitor with a plaque dedicated in 1996 by the Friends of the Libraries USA.

Stevens enjoyed the good life that his profession as an insurance executive afforded and wrote of his enchantment with the Casa Marina in a letter to his wife: "This is one of the choicest places I've been to. The place is paradise."

The hotel has undergone a series of incarnations since its opening. During World War II the Casa Marina served as officers' quarters for the US Navy; during the Cuban Missile Crisis it became an army installation. Its glory days ended during the Great Depression, but the hotel recovered its reputation in the 1990s with a $43 million renovation and expansion. Today this grand hotel offers 311 guest rooms and a host of amenities including swimming, tennis, golf, and outings arranged for guests. It is convenient to Duval Street and all of the major Key West attractions while still providing an air of elegance and Old World style. It remains one of Florida's most treasured historic hotels.

Casa Marina, 1500 Reynolds Street, Key West, FL 33040 (305-296-3535; www.casamarinaresort.com)

ᙅ Miami

FLORIDA'S LARGEST AND MOST COSMOPOLITAN CITY has in recent years become a glamorous getaway for the Hollywood set. But before the days of South Beach and its prized Art Deco District, Miami was a quiet seaside destination that attracted a range of writers and artists. Its azure-blue skies and brilliant sunsets were trademarks of the seaport city. In the early 1930s and early '40s Miami became the residence of poet Robert Frost and early environmentalist Marjory Stoneman Douglas. Its literary legacy continues today—among its best-known current authors are Carl Hiaasen (*Striptease*) and Elmore Leonard (*Get Shorty*).

ROBERT FROST'S PENCIL PINES

Poet Robert Frost, born in California and educated in New England, traveled to Miami to escape the harsh New England winters. Following several visits to the Sunshine State, Frost purchased Pencil Pines. Listed on the National Register of Historic Places, the appealing 5-acre lot holds an understated residence reminiscent of a quaint New England cottage. Frost owned the house until 1963, describing it as a "New England cottage . . . simple, utilitarian and screened in from the world by heavy foliage. The cottage is in a place with a yard full of fruit trees, avocadoes and mango." Now privately owned, Pencil Pines features a plaque commemorating the poet's residence.

One of Florida's most ardent environmentalists was Marjory Stoneman Douglas, author of *The Everglades: River of Grass*. Published in 1947, the book was released the same year that the Everglades National Park was dedicated. Douglas moved to Miami to work for the *Miami Herald* before becoming a freelance writer. Focusing national attention on the Everglades became her consuming passion and mission. Her book on the Everglades, which advocated for saving of the fragile ecosystem, was an instant best-seller. "There are no other Everglades in the world," she maintained, pointing to the region's importance as the only subtropical preserve in North America. Thanks largely to her diligent efforts, for which she was awarded the Medal of Freedom, this geographic treasure has become one of Florida's most visited attractions.

Douglas's former Coconut Grove cottage is located at 3744–3754 Stewart Avenue. Built between 1924 and 1926, the house is where she resided for more than 70 years and produced the majority of her writings, including *The Everglades: River of Grass.* In April 2007 the cottage, on the National Register of Historic Places, became part of the Florida Park Service, with hopes that one day it would be restored and open to the public. Stoneman's most powerful legacy is found at the Everglades National Park (see "Excursions and Diversions"). Today these breathtaking wetlands are one of the most unusual geographic features in the United States and home to a bevy of bird life, including wood storks, white ibis, roseate spoonbills, egrets, Audubon's shearwater, and the surf scoter. This is also one of the few remaining places where the elusive and endangered Florida panther is found.

🐚 LITERARY LODGING

THE BILTMORE HOTEL

Just southwest of downtown Miami in the lovely city of Coral Gables is the historic and luxurious Biltmore Hotel. Flanked by wide lawns, the main hotel, with its Mediterranean architecture, recalls a forgotten era in Miami's history. Its spiraling tower is reminiscent of the Giralda in Seville, Spain. Hand-painted frescoes on barrel-vaulted ceilings make the Biltmore one of Florida's most distinctive hotels.

Built by developer George Merrick in 1924, the Biltmore, a National Historic Landmark, has appealed to everyone from gangsters to golfers. When it opened for business on January 14, 1926, champagne flowed freely for guests as they danced the night away to the music of the Paul Whiteman Orchestra. Al Capone was one of the hotel's most prominent guests. The flamboyant gangster appreciated the finer things in life, and at the Biltmore he found them. He lived in the Everglades Suite—now renamed the Al Capone Suite—when he retired from his day job. The story goes that during Prohibition, Capone's lackey, Thomas "Fatty" Walsh, ran a speakeasy from the suite on the 13th floor. But Capone and his cronies were not the only ones to enjoy the Biltmore's amenities. The Duke and Duchess of Windsor, Judy Garland, Clark Gable, *Tarzan* star Johnny Weissmuller, and President Franklin Roosevelt, among other luminaries, stayed here.

With the arrival of the Great Depression and World War II, however, the hotel's glory days seemed a distant memory. In 1942 the hotel was converted into a military hospital; it later became the University of Miami's Medical School. In 1973 all this changed when the venerable landmark was transferred to the city of Coral Gables. Ten years later the first phase of its restoration began. Re-opened in 1987 following a $55 million renovation, Merrick's dream is alive today with a spa, four restaurants, and an 18-hole golf course designed by Donald Ross.

The Biltmore Hotel, 1200 Anastasia Avenue, Coral Gables (855-311-6903; www.biltmorehotel.com)

⚙ EXCURSIONS AND DIVERSIONS

EVERGLADES NATIONAL PARK

To fully appreciate what Marjory Stoneman Douglas accomplished in her book *The Everglades: River of Grass,* head out to this geographic treasure roughly 45 minutes from Miami. Visiting this, one of the most unusual ecosystems in the world, will ensure that you are seeing the best of Florida. Spanning the southern tip of the Florida peninsula, the park's 1.5 million acres mark the only subtropical preserve in North America. This wonder is home to a bevy of birdlife, and is the habitat of the elusive and endangered Florida panther. It is also one of the few places on the planet where alligators and crocodiles live together in the water environment.

Ranger-led activities, kayaking, canoeing, and fishing await visitors to this amazing ecosystem. You can also opt to take a narrated boat tour from the **Gulf Coast Visitor Center** in Everglades City, skimming along the shimmering waters. Be on the lookout for wildlife and bird life on this venture. At the **Royal Palm Visitor Center,** you can take part in the Anhinga Amble, a 50-minute guided trek along a raised boardwalk, possibly seeing alligators and an array of birds up close and personal.

Everglades National Park, 40001 State Highway 9336, Homestead, FL 33034 (305-242-7700; www.nps.gov/ever)

⤳ Tampa

Nothing could have held him back . . . he was ready to swim the ocean.
—JOSEPH CONRAD

AT THE HEIGHT OF THE GILDED AGE, Henry Plant, a newly minted millionaire who had amassed a fortune in railroads, built Tampa's most opulent hotel, the Tampa Bay, at a cost of $2.5 million. Known as "Plant's palace," the Moorish Revival structure resembled a resort, offering guests every amenity imaginable, from tennis to sailing, rowing to rickshaw rides. Exotic furnishings, Venetian-style mirrors, sumptuous decorations, and great balconies, verandas, and piazzas accented the unusual silver-tipped minarets that framed its exterior.

All that changed with the outbreak of the Spanish-American War in 1898. Plant, a close friend of Colonel Teddy Roosevelt, convinced Secretary of War Russell Alger that Tampa was an ideal staging ground for troops on their way to Cuba. Soldiers could easily load from the city's excellent port facilities onto Plant's steamships en route to the conflict.

Overnight the lavish hotel was transformed into headquarters for Roosevelt's Rough Riders. With the new mission came an influx of renowned journalists such as Stephen Crane and Richard Harding Davis. While khaki-attired troops trained and occupied the plush hotel, Crane and Davis along with other reporters spent their time in the hotel's Reading and Writing Room.

Crane, who had narrowly escaped a shipwreck off Florida's coast just two years earlier (see the "Daytona Beach" section), befriended fellow journalist Davis while in Tampa. Crane had arrived in Tampa via New York and Key West to work for Joseph Pulitzer's World Syndicate. His passions for reporting and for adventure became hallmarks of his life and career as a correspondent. In a letter to a friend published in the 1900 edition of the *New York Times,* Crane wrote: "The one thing that deeply pleases me in my literary life—brief and inglorious as it is—is the fact that men of sense believe me to be sincere. As far as myself and my own meager success are concerned, I began the battle of life with no talent, no equipment, but an ardent admiration and desire. . . . When I ought to have been at recitations I was studying faces on the streets, and when I ought to have been studying my next day's lessons I was watching the trains roll in and out of the Central Station."

There's much more information on Crane's involvement with the war and his time in Tampa at the **Henry B. Plant Museum** in the former Tampa Bay Hotel (now part of the University of Tampa campus). The building has been artfully restored to reflect Crane's era. Literary visitors will especially want to see the Reading and Writing Room. Inlaid wainscoting, expansive windows, rare books, vintage newspapers and magazines, and the inkstands that Crane and Harding used all create an 1890s atmosphere. You can also view archival photographs and learn more about this historic structure.

THE READING AND WRITING ROOM AT THE HENRY B. PLANT MUSEUM
Courtesy of the Henry B. Plant Museum

The mission to Cuba would be Crane's last as a war correspondent, but important pieces of his career in literature and journalism remain behind at the museum. Outside the building is a plaque mentioning Roosevelt, the Rough Riders, and the Spanish-American War.

> **Henry B. Plant Museum,** 401 West Kennedy Boulevard, Tampa, FL 33606 (813-254-1891; www.plantmuseum.com)

🕯 LITERARY LODGING

HISTORIC TAMPA ACCOMMODATIONS

The **Renaissance Vinoy Resort & Golf Club** is a splashy, grand hotel overlooking Tampa Bay. It is not known for certain whether Scott Fitzgerald and Ernest Hemingway met here for cocktails, but the anecdote sure adds to the allure of this towering salmon-colored structure. Wealthy Pennsylvania businessman Aymer Vinoy Laughner put up the initial investment and recruited architect Henry Taylor to design the 375-room property, which opened in 1925.

The Mediterranean Revival hotel is listed on the National Register of Historic Places and part of the National Trust's Historic Hotels Group. When the building was threatened with demolition in 1992, the Marriott Renaissance Group stepped up to provide a multimillion-dollar face-lift. Everyone from actor Jimmy Stewart to baseball great Babe Ruth and golfer Walter Hagan has stayed at the Vinoy. Its amenities include an 18-hole golf course, a marina, 12 Har-Tru tennis courts, and two swimming pools. The Clubhouse at the golf course features architectural pieces brought over from St. Petersburg, Russia, in 1925 to replicate an open-air market complete with minarets and onion domes.

The **Don CeSar Hotel** overlooking Tampa Bay dates back to 1928. Known as the "Pink Palace," the Don CeSar resembles a Mediterranean castle. Public areas recall the Gatsby era, while many rooms offer views of the Gulf of Mexico or Boca Ciega Bay. The AAA Four-Diamond property offers two beachfront pools, Spa Oceana, and 7 miles of powdery white-sand beaches.

The Renaissance Vinoy Hotel Resort & Golf Club, 501 5th Avenue Northeast, St. Petersburg, FL (727-894-1000; www.marriott.com)

The Don CeSar Hotel, 3400 Gulf Boulevard, St. Petersburg, FL 33706 (727-360-1881; www.loweshotels.com/doncesar)

✿ EXCURSIONS AND DIVERSIONS

EXPLORING TAMPA

Pirates and buccaneers once plied these waters. Following your Crane excursion at the Henry Plant Museum, some additional outings could include the **Florida Aquarium,** which dominates Tampa's waterfront area. Adventures include a wild dolphin cruise aboard a 72-foot powered catamaran.

For art enthusiasts the **Salvador Dali Museum** in nearby St. Petersburg is another great choice. The museum houses the largest collection of Dali paintings outside Spain. It was designed by Yann Weymouth Hok. You're greeted at the entranceway with a large free-form geodesic dome and a helical staircase. This unusual architectural detail coils up two and three-quarter rotations from the base, making the architecture as striking and unusual as Dali's paintings. The collection consists of 96 oil paintings, original drawings, books, manuscripts, and photographs of Dali. A 95-seat theater for film presentations and seminars along with the Avant Gardens make this one of the country's most original and exciting museums.

The Florida Aquarium, 701 Channelside Drive, Tampa, FL 33602 (813-273-4000; wwwflaquarium.org)

The Salvador Dali Museum, 1 Dali Boulevard, St. Petersburg, FL 33701 (727-823-3767; www.thedali.org)

～ Venice

> *He was a giant of a horse, glistening black—too big to be pure Arabian. His mane was like a crest, mounting, then falling low. His neck was long and slender, and arched to the small, savagely beautiful head. The head was that of the wildest of all wild creatures—a stallion born wild—and it was beautiful, savage, and splendid. A stallion with a wonderful physical perfection that matched his savage, ruthless spirit.*
>
> —WALTER FARLEY, *The Black Stallion*

FOR ANY HORSE ENTHUSIAST or fan of classic children's literature, Walter Farley's *Black Stallion* stories remain at the top of the list of favorites. Farley's profound love of horses—as a result of working with his uncle, a professional horseman and trainer—led him to begin writing the first drafts of *The Black Stallion* while in high school. He was encouraged by a Columbia University professor. He submitted the final manuscript to Random House and the first *Black Stallion* book was published in 1946, when Farley was 26. Following a stint as an advertising copywriter in New York and writing for *Yank Magazine* during World War II, Farley continued his stories. Ultimately he authored more than 30 books in his literary career, with 15 devoted to the *Black Stallion* series. "Imagination," he wrote, "can help you reach into the heavens to grasp an idea, bring it down to earth, and make it work."

Dividing his time between Venice, Florida, and Earlville, Pennsylvania, Farley and his wife, Rosemary, were pivotal in founding the Friends of the Venice Public Library in 1962; the **Walter Farley Wing of the Venice Public Library** includes a permanent display on Farley and his contributions to children's literature, as well as a plaque dedicated in 1989 by the

Friends of the Libraries USA. In 1979 a film version of *The Black Stallion* was released, followed by *The Black Stallion Returns* in 1983.

Venice Public Library, 300 South Nokomis Avenue, Venice, FL 34285 (941-861-1330; www.sclibs.net)

§ LITERARY LODGING

THE GASPARILLA INN & CLUB

Approximately one hour from Venice is the Gasparilla Inn & Club. Named after the pirate Jose Gaspar, the inn dates back to 1913 and is a member of the National Trust's Historic Hotels Group. With a white-pillared entrance, pale wooden frame, and Victorian-style roofs overlooking both the Gulf of Mexico and Charlotte Harbor, the inn is set on 180 acres in Boca Grande. Stepping inside this hotel is reminiscent of visiting another era. The Du Ponts, Henry Plant, and artist John Singer Sargent are among its former guests.

Sport fishing, kayaking, cycling, or taking any number of excursions from the hotel make this stop a memorable one. Privately owned, the resort exudes Old World elegance.

The Gasparilla Inn, 500 Palm Avenue, Boca Grande, FL 33901 (941-964-4500; www.the-gasparilla-inn.com)

ᕧ **Wabasso**

The right to feel at home in one's own home-place seemed to open the whole world of homes to one, to turn into a right to feel at home in other places, besides—to lead one's mind, and one's feet, one's life, into the lives of others. . . . I am telling, I believe, the true story of human residence in the habitat of nature, the universe in which earth is the human address.

—LAURA RIDING JACKSON, "HOME"

POET LAURA RIDING JACKSON, associated with the Fugitives from Vanderbilt University—which included Robert Penn Warren, John Crowe Ransom, and Allen Tate—settled in this remote corner of Florida in 1943. Much like Marjorie Kinnan Rawlings, who traveled to Cross Creek to write and cultivate an orange grove, Jackson moved here to both manage a grapefruit grove and work on her writings.

North of Vero Beach, Jackson and her husband Schuyler lived in stark simplicity in the cottage. When the Jacksons lived in the house, they had no heat, phone, or electricity. Built in 1910 in the cracker style, the cottage served as Jackson's home until her death in 1991. In 1994 the house was moved from its original location for preservation purposes, and is now found on the grounds of the **Environmental Learning Center** off State Road 510. Managed by the **Laura Riding Jackson Foundation,** it is open for tours Saturday mornings from October to May.

The house remains largely as it was when Jackson lived there and contains her original belongings. It now serves as an arts center. A plaque was dedicated in 1995 by the Friends of the Libraries USA and pays tribute to the writer with the simple words, "The most consistently good woman poet of all time."

> **Environmental Learning Center,** 255 Live Oak Drive, Vero Beach, FL 32961

> **Laura Riding Jackson Foundation,** PO Box 6728, Vero Beach, FL 32961 (772-569-6718; www.lauraridingjackson.com)

CHAPTER
3

GEORGIA

THE LARGEST STATE EAST OF THE MISSISSIPPI RIVER, Georgia has an indomitable spirit that radiates from its capital city, Atlanta, the proud symbol of the New South.

Once reduced to ashes during the Civil War, Atlanta played a critical role in the civil rights movement. The Reverend Dr. Martin Luther King Jr. was born in Atlanta in 1929, and used his lectern at the city's Ebenezer Baptist Church to outline his visionary hopes for the nation's future, making Georgia the South's beacon.

The Civil War and civil rights movement were watershed moments in Georgia's history. As a literary locale, the state serves up a wealth of sites and a diverse collection of writers. Margaret Mitchell's *Gone with the Wind,* Sidney Lanier's "Song of the Chattahoochee," Eugene O'Neill's *Ah, Wilderness!,* James Dickey's *Deliverance,* and Carson McCullers's *The Heart Is a Lonely Hunter* are all part of Georgia's rich range of works.

John Berendt's *Midnight in the Garden of Good and Evil* immediately brings to mind the mysterious beauty of Savannah. Flannery O'Connor's ancestral home in Milledgeville is where she wrote most of her important works. Conrad Aiken's Georgia memories are central to his writings.

From its cities to its barrier islands, small towns, and rural outposts, an excursion through Georgia holds great promise for literary travelers.

ᜈ᜵ Athens

> There was a South of slavery and secession—that South is dead. There
> is a South of union and freedom—that South, thank God, is living,
> breathing, growing every hour.
>
> —HENRY GRADY, QUOTING BENJAMIN H. HILL,
> "THE NEW SOUTH" SPEECH, BOSTON, 1886

LOVELY VISTAS OF DOGWOODS, camellias, and azaleas accent the pastoral setting of the University of Georgia, conjuring up images of the Old
South.

One of the most influential and visionary journalists of the post–
Civil War period was *Atlanta Journal Constitution* editor Henry Grady. Born
in Athens in 1850, Grady, who earned his reputation as a leading propo-
nent of the New South movement with his daring editorials, is honored
at several Athens sites. A bust of Grady is found in the library of UGA's
College of Journalism and Mass Communication; an annual tradition at
the **Grady College** has students adorning the bust with a cap to celebrate
his birthday. A short distance from the campus is the **Taylor-Grady
House,** where Grady lived with his mother and sister while attending the
University of Georgia from 1865 until 1868.

A striking Greek Revival mansion listed on the National Register of
Historic Places, the house was purchased by his father, Major William S.
Grady, in 1863, while on leave from the Confederate army; William was
later killed in the Battle of Petersburg. The home became Grady's residence
while attending the University of Georgia. Grady referred to the house as
"an old southern home, with its lofty pillars, and its white pigeons flut-
tering down through the golden air." It epitomizes the antebellum southern mansion; think Tara from *Gone with the Wind.*

The house was restored at a cost of $1.7 million to reflect the 1860s
era. Period pieces adorn its interior. It is owned by the City of Athens and
operated by the Junior League of Athens, and is open for self-guided tours.

The Taylor-Grady House, 634 Prince Avenue, Athens, GA
30601 (706-549-8688; www.taylorgradyhouse.com)

THE MARGARET MITCHELL COLLECTION

The University of Georgia's **Hargrett Rare Book and Manuscript Library** contains the largest repository of Margaret Mitchell material in the world. Individuals can arrange to view the prized collection, bequeathed to the university by Mitchell's family. Photographs, personal papers, and correspondence showcase Mitchell's versatility in both her writing and her life, from her flapper days to her journalism career and active Red Cross involvement during World War II. Other collections at the library include Erskine Caldwell, Randall Savage, and Lewis Grizzard.

Hargrett Library, Richard B. Russell Building, 300 South Hull Street, University of Georgia, Athens, GA 30602 (706-542-7123; www.libs .uga.edu/hargrett)

🖉 LITERARY LODGING

THE COLONELS

Picture *Gone with the Wind* with all of the luxurious amenities and period furnishings and you will have some idea what awaits visitors to this stately inn. Billed as "a distinguished country manor on Angel Oaks Farm," The Colonels is located 90 minutes from the center of Atlanta, deep in Scarlett O'Hara territory. Dating back to 1860, the inn's six rooms are decorated with period antiques and four-poster beds. Magnolia and pecan trees frame its resplendent setting, and if you prefer to ride your mount here, stables are available for overnight guests. "Set a spell" on the front portico, where white columns add to the ambience.

The Colonels, 3890 Barnett Shoals Road, Athens, GA 30605 (706-559-9595; www.thecolonels.net)

⊕ EXCURSIONS AND DIVERSIONS

STATE BOTANICAL GARDEN OF GEORGIA

Explore the Peach State's native flora at the State Botanical Garden. Opened in 1968 and part of the University of Georgia, the expansive gardens covering 313 acres can be enjoyed at your own pace or via guided tours. The Main Conservatory, Heritage Garden, and International Garden are the three main attractions. There is a visitors center and gift shop for browsing as well.

State Botanical Garden of Georgia, 2450 South Milledge Avenue, Athens, GA 30605 (706-542-1244; www.botgarden .uga.edu)

ᴥ Atlanta

I want to say to General Sherman . . . that from the ashes he left us in 1864 we have raised a brave and beautiful city; that somehow or other we have caught the sunshine in the bricks and mortar of our homes.
—HENRY GRADY, "THE NEW SOUTH," 1886

MARGARET MITCHELL
Courtesy of Atlanta History Center

GONE WITH THE WIND began in Margaret Mitchell's imagination long before its publication in 1936. An Atlanta girl born and bred, Mitchell spent her childhood steeped in the vivid stories of her ancestors: Her great-grandfather had emigrated from Ireland, eventually settling on a plantation near Jonesboro; her grandfather had fought in the Civil War.

Born in 1900, Mitchell attended an Atlanta finishing school before entering Smith College in 1918. A series of events caused her to leave Smith after her freshman year and return to Atlanta: Her fiancé was killed in World War I and she lost her mother to influenza. After a brief marriage in 1922 ended in annulment, she went to work for the *Atlanta Journal Sunday Magazine*, and wrote for the publication for four years.

Mitchell remarried in 1925 and lived with her husband in a first-floor apartment on Crescent Avenue that she referred to as "the Dump." It was in this apartment in 1926, while recuperating from a broken ankle, that she began her famous novel, which took ten years to complete. Originally titled "Tomorrow Is Another Day," its publication in 1936 took Atlanta and the country by storm. It sold a million copies in its first six months in print, and won the Pulitzer Prize the following year. The film adaptation, released in 1939, broke box-office records and is a classic of Hollywood's golden age.

The **Margaret Mitchell House** in the city's Midtown section opens a window on Atlanta's past and celebrates Mitchell's literary legacy. Built in 1899, the Tudor Revival house faces Peachtree Street and is surrounded by towering skyscrapers. Abandoned in 1978, it almost fell to the wrecking ball, until a group of preservationists stepped in to save the historic site in 1985. The house was opened to the public in 1997 at a cost of $5 million, funded by the Daimler-Benz Corp. Listed on the National Register of Historic Places, it attracts well over 50,000 visitors annually and is managed by the Atlanta History Center.

THE MARGARET MITCHELL HOUSE
Courtesy of Atlanta History Center

A tour of the house gives visitors fascinating insight into Mitchell's life and work. Vintage photographs of the author, including one of her interviewing Rudolph Valentino, adorn the walls of the galleries. Her desk from the *Atlanta Journal* is also on view. A carved lion head on a staircase banister, which found its way into her book, was a totem of sorts. Mitchell had a habit of rubbing the lion's nose when she passed, for good luck. The living room, kitchen, and bedroom are filled with period pieces, though none of the furnishings is original.

A photograph of Mitchell's grandfather in his Confederate uniform hangs on the wall in the living room of her small apartment. Her typewriter sits in a corner alcove of this room, where Mitchell went to work every day.

The success of Mitchell's book changed her life dramatically; though

MITCHELL'S TYPEWRITER
Courtesy of Atlanta History Center

it made her a wealthy woman, she was uncomfortable with the fame it brought. She continued to live in Atlanta, and she and her husband took up a variety of philanthropic causes benefiting the city.

Margaret Mitchell's life came to an abrupt end on August 16, 1949, five days after she was hit by a speeding motorist while crossing 13th and Peachtree Streets. She died at Grady Memorial Hospital and is buried at **Oakland Cemetery,**

MARGARET MITCHELL *Courtesy of Atlanta History Center*

founded in 1850 and one of Atlanta's most historic landmarks. On its hilltop setting is where General John B. Hood watched the Battle of Atlanta. It seems fitting that the writer who gave us the best-known Civil War novel found her last resting place alongside both Confederate and Federal soldiers.

The Mitchell story continues in nearby Jonesboro, home to the **Road to Tara Museum,** one of the most comprehensive collections of *Gone with the Wind* movie memorabilia in the country. Located about 15 miles south of Atlanta via I-75, Clayton County lays claim to being the birthplace of the novel and is where you can find the antebellum plantation that was the model for Mitchell's Tara.

The museum is located in Jonesboro's restored 1867 rail depot. This diverse collection of *Gone with the Wind* memorabilia includes replicas of some of the costumes from the film as well as Margaret Mitchell's china. The *Gone with the Wind* tour that departs from the museum details Mitchell's connection to Jonesboro and its influences on her famous novel.

Another Mitchell stop is in Marietta, about 30 miles north of Atlanta, where the **Gone with the Wind Museum: Scarlett on the Square** holds special interest for fans of the novel and film.

Margaret Mitchell House, 990 Peachtree Street, Atlanta, GA 30309 (404-249-7015; www.margaretmitchellhouse.com)

Oakland Cemetery, 248 Oakland Avenue SE, Atlanta, GA 30312 (404-688-2107; www.oaklandcemetery.com)

Road to Tara Museum, 104 North Main Street, Jonesboro, GA 30236 (770-478-4800; www.visitscarlett.com)

Marietta Gone with the Wind Museum: Scarlett on the Square, 18 Whitlock Avenue, Marietta, GA 30064 (770-794-5576; www.gwtwmarietta.com)

JOEL CHANDLER HARRIS

Another major Atlanta literary landmark is **The Wren's Nest,** Joel Chandler Harris's home. Harris, a journalist with the *Atlanta Journal Constitution* for 24 years and creator of the Uncle Remus tales, lived in the Queen Anne Victorian home from 1881 to 1908.

Named Wren's Nest because a family of wrens took up residence in the mailbox, the house displays intricate latticework and a breezy veranda where Harris, regarded as Georgia's Aesop for his creation of animal characters such as Br'er Rabbit and Br'er Fox, would sit and read to his children. The house is a National and City of Atlanta Historic Landmark.

Courtesy of the Wren's Nest

Inside the house, vintage family heirlooms, books (including first editions of the works of Mark Twain), photographs (including one signed by Teddy Roosevelt), and furnishings that belonged to the upper-middle-class Harris family are on view. His life in the house revolved around his family, reading, writing, and storytelling.

The writer's bedroom remains as he left it. A black felt fedora, reading glasses, and the typewriter he used to compose his Uncle Remus tales are on the bedside table. Every Saturday at the house, the Wren's Nest Ramblers tell their favorite Uncle Remus tales. During the Christmas holidays, the home is bedecked in Victorian splendor.

The Wren's Nest, 1050 Ralph David Abernathy Boulevard SW, Atlanta, GA 30310 (404-753-7735; www.wrensnestonline.com)

LITERARY LODGING

GEORGIAN TERRACE HOTEL

Atlanta's Georgian Terrace Hotel certainly looks like a place with literary connections. And indeed it has them. The 1911 Beaux-Arts landmark is just a few blocks from the apartment where Margaret Mitchell wrote *Gone with the Wind.* The story goes that an editor with Macmillan named Latham was traveling through the South looking for manuscripts. Mitchell met him at a luncheon and showed him around the city, denying she had a book for his consideration. But on the last day of his stay, she walked to the Georgian Terrace, where

GEORGIAN TERRACE HOTEL

Latham was staying, and handed over her manuscript, reputedly saying, "Take the damn thing before I change my mind"—or words to that effect.

Throughout its storied history the Georgian Terrace has gone through several incarnations but retains its Old World elegance, particularly in the Grand Ballroom, where on December 15, 1939, the lavish film-premiere party for *Gone with the Wind* was held. The film's stars Clark Gable and Vivien Leigh, along with Carole Lombard, Laurence Olivier, Louis B. Mayer, David O. Selznick, and Margaret Mitchell, were all in attendance for the glamorous event.

Added to the National Register of Historic Places in 1986, the hotel is one of Atlanta's most recognizable historical landmarks. At the Peachtree entrance, a Georgia Historical Marker commemorates the hotel's ties to Mitchell and *Gone with the Wind*.

It is across from the Fox Theatre, another of Atlanta's historic landmarks, and close to the Atlanta metro's Midtown stop.

Georgian Terrace Hotel, 659 Peachtree Street NE, Atlanta, GA 30308 (404-897-1991; www.thegeorgianterrace.com)

❋ EXCURSIONS AND DIVERSIONS

EXPLORING ATLANTA

The South's largest and most cosmopolitan city is abundant with cultural outings and offerings, several of which relate to Mitchell, the Battle of Atlanta, and the history of the city.

The **Atlanta History Center** on West Paces Ferry Road chronicles Atlanta's past with photographs, maps, and Civil War artifacts. The Swan House is the highlight at this site. The 1928 estate of Edward Hamilton Inman has formal gardens, terraced lawns, ivy arches, and waterfalls. The Swan House Tea Room is an ideal place to take a break from your Mitchell excursion, with the mile-long Swan Woods Trail one of the prettiest in Atlanta.

To learn more about the Battle of Atlanta that played such a significant role in Mitchell's book, head out to the **Cyclorama and Civil War Museum** in Grant Park. Created in the 1880s, the 360-degree cylindrical painting is 42 feet high and vividly depicts the Battle of Atlanta, July 22, 1864. In the 1970s an $11 million restoration preserved the historical painting. Narrated and enhanced by music and sound effects, the painting brings to life the battle and General John B. Hood's desperate attempt to block General William Tecumseh Sherman's march into Atlanta. A display case of Civil War arms, paintings, and portraits of both the Union and Confederate leaders makes this an excellent addition to your Atlanta Civil War excursion.

For a look into former President Jimmy Carter, an author in his own right, head out to Highland Avenue just outside the city and visit the **Jimmy Carter Library & Museum,** one of the country's finest presidential libraries. Situated on 30 acres of gardens, lakes, and waterfalls, the center houses a comprehensive collection documenting Carter's White House years including 1.5 million photographs and several hours of audio- and videotapes. An exact replica of the Oval Office with Carter describing his White House years adds to the experience. Also of interest is a collection on display of "gifts of state" given to Carter during his presidency. Carter is known to drop by the museum throughout the year for seminars, book signings, and special programs.

The Atlanta History Center, Swan House, 130 West Paces Ferry Road, Atlanta, GA 30305 (404-814-4000; www.atlantahistory center.com)

The Jimmy Carter Library & Museum, 441 Freedom Parkway, Atlanta, GA 30307 (404-865-7100; www.jimmycarterlibrary.gov)

Atlanta Cyclorama, 800 Cherokee Avenue SE, Atlanta, GA 30315 (404-658-7625; www.atlantacyclorama.org)

∾ Columbus

> *The town had not known a winter as cold as this one for years. Frost*
> *formed on the windowpanes and whitened the roofs of houses. The winter*
> *afternoons glowed with a hazy lemon light and shadows were a delicate*
> *blue. A thin coat of ice crusted the puddles in the streets, and it was said*
> *on the day after Christmas that only ten miles to the north there was a*
> *light fall of snow.*
>
> —CARSON MCCULLERS,
> *The Heart Is a Lonely Hunter*

AN ORIGINAL IN EVERY SENSE OF THE WORD, Lula Carson Smith was born into a middle-class family in Columbus, Georgia. Overlooking the Chattahoochee River, Columbus, 100 miles south of Atlanta, was of primary importance during the Civil War, with "King Cotton" cotton fueling its prosperity.

McCullers began her creative journey by studying piano at age 13. Soon thereafter she discovered the powerful literary voices of Chekhov and Tolstoy, awakening her desire to become a writer. Meeting playwright Eugene O'Neill at the local library enhanced her literary aspirations.

"In our old Georgia home," she wrote, "we used to have two sitting rooms—a back one and a front one—with folding doors between. These were the family living rooms and the theatre of my shows. The front sitting room was an auditorium, the back sitting room the stage. The sliding doors the curtain."

The novelist responsible for penning *The Ballad of the Sad Café, The Member of the Wedding,* and *The Heart Is a Lonely Hunter* traveled on a steamer at age 17 from Savannah to New York. McCullers soon began submitting stories to *Vogue* and *Harper's Bazaar* magazines, but her desire to write a novel only intensified in New York. At age 23 McCullers completed her first novel, *The Heart Is a Lonely Hunter,* published in 1946.

The Georgia writer had an uncanny knack for blending personal stories and experiences into her books. "I become the person I am writing about," she said when queried about her writing style. Her poignant stories of growing up, lost souls, and searchers continue to enthrall readers. A close friend of playwright Tennessee Williams—who regarded her as the "greatest prose writer the South has ever produced"—McCullers never considered herself a southern writer, but many of her recurring themes clearly identify her as one.

Columbus celebrates the author's connections at several sites with the primary one being the **Carson McCullers Center,** her childhood home. The center's **Smith-McCullers House Museum** displays a collection of personal artifacts, photographs, and archival material related to her life and writing career. Operated by Columbus State University, the house is where the Smith family lived from 1925 until 1944. Located in the Wildwood Circle/Hillcrest District, it is open to the public by appointment; allow at least 24 hours' notice in arranging a tour.

Other McCullers stops should include **Columbus High School,** from which she graduated at age 16 and which features a display case devoted to her and her writings in the lobby area; and the **Columbus State University Archives,** which house many of her notebooks and writings.

Carson McCullers Center, 1519 Stark Avenue, Columbus, GA 31906 (706-565-4021; www.mccullerscenter.org)

Columbus High School, 1700 Cherokee Avenue, Columbus, GA 31906 (706-748-2534; www.columbushighga.org)

Columbus State University Archives, Simon Schwob Memorial Library, 4225 University Avenue, Columbus, GA 31907 (706-507-8672; http://archives.columbusstate.edu)

✿ EXCURSIONS AND DIVERSIONS

COLUMBUS HIGHLIGHTS

Georgia's third largest city is an ideal place to experience both the Chattahoochee River so familiar to McCullers, and the Civil War naval history associated with the area.

Riverwalk is one of the newest additions to the town's downtown area and a great place to wander along the river and enjoy Columbus. The 15-mile linear park that follows the banks of the Chattahoochee is abundant with cafés, shops, and outdoor activities.

The Port Columbus **National Civil War Naval Museum** is a 40,000-square-foot facility featuring an outstanding collection of historic items. Uniforms, Civil War artifacts, and equipment used by both the Union and Confederate soldiers are on display in this dazzling museum.

Columbus Convention & Visitors Bureau, 900 Front Avenue, Columbus, GA 31902, 706-322-1613; 1-800-999-1613; www.visitcolumbusga.com

National Civil War Naval Museum, 1002 Victory Drive, Columbus, GA 31901 (706-327-9798; http://portcolumbus.org)

Eatonton

I infused The Color Purple *with all of my own feelings, and I joined gleefully with my ancestors and with my parents because I had learned as a little girl a lot of the stories of their lives. So that I could almost play those lives and enjoy them—and at the same time dream the endings.*

—ALICE WALKER

EATONTON IS THE BIRTHPLACE of Alice Walker (best known for *The Color Purple*) and Joel Chandler Harris (author of the Uncle Remus tales). The town plays homage to both writers at a host of sites.

Both Walker and Harris reached back into their childhoods to write their stories. The **Uncle Remus Museum** is located in Turner Park, three blocks south of the courthouse on Highway 441. This was the homestead of Joseph Addison Turner, constructed of pine logs from the original Putnam County slave cabins. The stories and characters of the Uncle Remus stories are captured in shadow boxes displaying carvings of the characters in the book. Inside the small museum are two photographs from the movie *Song of the South* and first editions of Harris's works.

Walker's novel *The Color Purple*, awarded the Pulitzer Prize in 1983, was based entirely on her life in Eatonton. Walker, the youngest of eight children, was born here in 1944. Memories of her grandparents' stories inspired her novel. Walker attended Atlanta's Spellman College and graduated from Sarah Lawrence, but her passion for reading and writing began in her Georgia hometown.

Following the success of *The Color Purple*, which was later adapted into a motion picture and Broadway production, Walker reflected on her literary life. "One thing I try to have in my life," she said, "is an awareness of and openness to mystery, which to me, is deeper than any politics, race or geographical location."

In 2002 Walker was inducted into the Georgia Writers Hall of Fame. Emory University acquired a portion of her papers in 2007. The **Alice Walker Driving Tour** takes travelers to many of the landmarks associated with the novel, including the Wards Chapel AME Church she attended as a child and the cemetery where her parents are interred. Tour information is available at the Eatonton Chamber of Commerce.

Uncle Remus Museum, 214 Oak Street, Eatonton, GA 31024 (706-485-6856; www.uncleremusmuseum.org)

Eatonton-Putnam Chamber of Commerce, 305 N. Madison Avenue, Eatonton, GA 31024 (706-485-7701; www.eatonton .com)

ᏝᎦ Macon

> *Look off, dear love, across the shallow sands,*
> *And mark yon meeting of the sun and sea,*
> *How long they kiss in sight of all the lands,*
> *Ah! longer, longer, we.*
>
> —SIDNEY LANIER, "AN EVENING SONG"

THE SOUTHERNMOST STOP on Georgia's Antebellum Trail is Macon. Endless avenues of Greek Revival architecture, wide vistas, and a proliferation of cherry blossoms make this one of the most bucolic destinations on a Georgia literary excursion. Over 50 buildings and homes here have been recognized for their architectural merit with a listing in the National Register of Historic Places.

Sidney Lanier, one of the South's most revered and respected poets, was born in Macon in 1842 at his grandfather's High Street cottage in the heart of Macon's historic district. The **Sidney Lanier Cottage** is now open for tours and operated by the Historic Macon Foundation; it is where you will find an imposing oak tree reminiscent of one of Lanier's most famous poems, "The Marshes of Glynn." Artifacts detailing his life and his writings are on display, including the silver alto flute he played with Baltimore's Peabody Symphony and first editions of his works. Family photographs adorn the interior, flanked by period furnishings.

THE SIDNEY LANIER COTTAGE
Courtesy of the Macon-Bibb County Convention & Visitors Bureau

Lanier experienced a traditional southern upbringing, where art, music, and literature played an important part in his development as a poet. His father, Robert, a lawyer, and mother, Mary Anderson, infused in him as a youth the importance of culture. Lanier was one of the first in Macon to enlist with the Confederacy and the Georgia Battalion. As a solder he worked as a blockade-runner off the coast of Wilmington, North Carolina, where he was ultimately captured and imprisoned at Point Lookout, Maryland. But it was during his imprisonment that he wrote "Tiger Lilies" and realized his literary voice.

Following the Civil War he spent several years working at his father's law firm, but his creative instincts took hold and he seriously began writing for magazines. Eventually Lanier traveled to Baltimore, where he lectured at Johns Hopkins University and played the flute with the Peabody Symphony. Some of his most beloved poems, including "Song of the Chattahoochee," "The Marshes of Glynn," and "The Crystal," all echo southern themes. Most of his poems were published posthumously by his widow.

Lanier's name graces several geographic features in Georgia, including Lanier Lake in central Georgia and the Sidney Lanier Bridge in Brunswick—the largest bridge named in honor of a poet. The oak tree by the edge of the water where he once relaxed is named Lanier Oak and can be seen on Highway 17 north of Gloucester Street, where a Georgia Historical Marker is found.

Sidney Lanier Cottage, 935 High Street, Macon, GA 31201 (478-742-5084; www.historicmacon.org/sidney-lanier-cottage)

⚜ LITERARY LODGING

1842 INN

If you are seeking to experience a genuine Old South inn, then the 1842 Inn should be at the top of your list. The former home of Macon mayor and cotton merchant John Gresham, the AAA Four-Diamond inn offers 19 rooms, all displaying the tastes and graciousness of the South. Heart-of-pine floors and 12-foot ceilings add to its atmosphere of a fine southern home. One of the inn's largest rooms is named after Sidney Lanier and evokes a literary ambience with its alcove setting.

1842 Inn, 353 College Street, Macon, GA 31201 (478-741-1842; www.1842inn.com)

✥ EXCURSIONS AND DIVERSIONS

MACON'S BLOOMS

Macon is home to the largest **Cherry Blossom Festival** outside of Washington, DC. More than 300,000 Yoshino cherry trees accent Macon's abundance of antebellum architecture. During this 10-day springtime event, the color pink takes over the city: Residents place pink wreaths on their doors and mailboxes, adding to the loveliness of Macon. Concerts and tours take place.

Another choice for enjoying the South's garden splendor is to take Macon's annual **Secret Garden Tour** to soak up southern scenery. The tour includes a visit to the Hay House, a National Historic Landmark.

Cherry Blossom Festival (478-751-7429; www.cherryblossom .com)

Hay House, 934 Georgia Avenue, Macon, GA (478-742-8155; www.maconga.org or www.georgiatrust.org)

ᕬ Milledgeville

> *The great advantage of being a southern writer is that we don't have to go anywhere to look for manners; bad or good; we've got them in abundance. We in the South live in a society that is rich in contradictions; rich in irony; rich in contrast; and particularly rich in its speech.*
> —FLANNERY O'CONNOR, "WRITING SHORT STORIES"

FLANNERY O'CONNOR'S LIFE PATH began in Savannah, where she was born in 1925, and continued in rural Milledgeville at **Andalusia,** the family's ancestral estate, which she called home beginning in 1938. She left

Andalusia for college, and there would be intermittent stops in Iowa, Connecticut, and New York along the way, but the Milledgeville farm is where she lived following a diagnosis of lupus at age 25, and is also where she completed the majority of her most significant works.

Listed on the National Register of Historic Places, the 544-acre Andalusia estate consists of the main house, a peafowl aviary, the main cow barn, and three tenant houses. The main house is a two-story plantation-style home built in 1850 and is where the author of *Wise Blood* and "A Good Man Is Hard to Find" lived from 1951 until her death in 1964.

In a letter to friend Ben Griffith she mentioned her farm and wrote, "We live four miles from Milledgeville on the road to Eatonton in a two-story farmhouse. The place is called Andalusia."

As you enter the house, which is on the outskirts of Milledgeville, you pass by a narrow hallway and see the dining room and the writer's bedroom, where she did all of her work. A desk, bookshelves, and the crutches she relied on so much for her independence are on view. Most of the furnishings in the house belonged to the writer, ensuring a personal perspective on her life. Most of her mornings were filled with writing while afternoons were reserved for greeting friends and tending to her large family of peacocks. In describing her literary life she wrote, "The writer operates at a peculiar crossroads where time and place and eternity somehow meet. His problem is to find that location."

Andalusia Farm is owned and managed by the **Flannery O'Connor— Andalusia Foundation** and remains one of Milledgeville's most visited sites. Tobler Creek bisects the farm and adds to its ambience. The pristine wilderness setting is home to white-tailed deer, red and gray foxes, and red-tailed hawks, making it a recommended respite after you explore O'-Connor's farm.

Additional landmarks and sites connected to O'Connor include a Georgia Historical Marker outside the entrance to Milledgeville on US Highway 441. At **Georgia State College,** her alma mater, the **Ina Dillard Russell Library** has a room devoted to her and her writings. O'Connor's mother began donating materials to the college in 1970. Over 700 books of her personal library as well as manuscript drafts for *Wise Blood* and her short stories are part of the collection. Photographs associated with her life at Andalusia are on view. The **Sacred Heart Catholic Church** on Jefferson Street is where she worshipped and bequeathed an endowment of

$200,000 upon her death. The writer is laid to rest at **Memory Hill Cemetery** at Liberty and Franklin Streets, making all of the key O'Connor sites within easy reach of one another.

Flannery O'Connor–Andalusia Foundation, PO Box 947, Milledgeville, GA 31059 (478-454-4029; www.andalusiafarm.org)

Ina Dillard Russell Library, 231 West Hancock Street, Milledgeville, GA 31061 (478-445-5004; www.library.gcsu.edu)

Memory Hill Cemetery, 300 West Franklin Street, Milledgeville, GA 31059 (www.friendsofcems.org/memoryhill)

Sacred Heart Catholic Church, 110 North Jefferson Street, Milledgeville, GA 31060 (478-452-2421; www.sacredheart milledgeville.com)

🍸 LITERARY LODGING

THE ANTEBELLUM INN

Georgia's former state capital is abundant with inns and antebellum architecture, but one clear standout for lodging is the Antebellum Inn in the heart of Milledgeville's historic district. Built in 1890, the white-columned Greek Revival inn offering five rooms and two parlors recalls a genteel southern home. Four-poster beds, a winding staircase, and wraparound porches with rocking chairs make this a thoroughly southern experience. A full southern breakfast that might include pecan waffles and scratch-made biscuits is included.

Antebellum Inn, 200 North Columbia Street, Milledgeville, GA 31061 (478-453-3993; www.antebelluminn.com)

⚙ EXCURSIONS AND DIVERSIONS

EXPLORING MILLEDGEVILLE

Discovering Georgia's former state capital is made easy if you hop a ride on the bright red trolley that scoots around to most of the town's major sites and attractions, including the Old Governor's Mansion and Lockerly Hall & Arboretum. Departing weekdays from the **Convention & Visitors Bureau,** the trolley is an ideal way to see the highlights of Milledgeville. The **Old Governor's Mansion** is a National Historic Landmark and a must-visit for seeing period antiques and learning more about the Peach State's history. In November 1864 General William Tecumseh Sherman was headquartered in the building on his "March to the Sea." **Lockerly Hall & Arboretum** is an 1852 Greek Revival mansion displaying period antiques; its 50-acre public garden showcases Georgia's plants and flowers along walking trails.

Milledgeville Convention & Visitors Bureau, 200 West Hancock Street, Milledgeville, GA 31061 (478-452-4687 or 800-653-1804; www.visitmilledgeville.org)

Old Governor's Mansion, 231 Hancock Street, Milledgeville, GA 31060 (478-445-4545; www.gcsu.edu/mansion)

Lockerly Hall & Arboretum, 1534 Irwinton Road, Milledgeville, GA 31061 (478-452-2112; www.locklery.gov)

ᔦ Moreland

In my view I'm just a subsidiary character to the whole process of writing. The only thing that really interests me is what I'm trying to make—the story itself that I'm trying to get told. That's it.

—ERSKINE CALDWELL

REGARDED AS THE SOUTH'S "literary bad boy," Erskine Caldwell was born in Moreland in 1903, the son of a Presbyterian minister and a schoolteacher. His Coweta County birthplace, **The Little Manse,** is about an hour's drive south of Atlanta. Caldwell's raw and bawdy language distinguished his style of writing in two of his most popular books, *Tobacco Road* and *God's Little Acre.* Caldwell was another one of editor Maxwell Perkins's finds; Perkins appreciated his honest portrayal of life in rural Georgia during the Great Depression. His books also caught the attention of Hollywood; *Tobacco Road* and *God's Little Acre* were both adapted for the big screen.

Caldwell began his literary journey at the *Atlanta Journal Constitution.* The three-room house where he was born is found on Camp Street but no longer open to the public.

Erskine Caldwell Birthplace, Camp Street, Moreland, GA 30259

∾ Savannah

Born in that most magical of cities, Savannah, I was allowed to run wild in the earthly paradise until I was nine; ideal for the boy who early decided he wanted to write.

—CONRAD AIKEN

MOSS-LADEN TREES arch over many of Savannah's historic squares, and the subtle scents of magnolias and gardenias permeate this southern destination. On most summer evenings soft breezes caress the city's riverfront and the 21 squares laid out by General James Oglethorpe in 1735. Like Charleston, its neighbor to the north, Savannah is one of the South's most distinctive destinations.

The city overlooks the flowing Savannah River, where barges once filled with cotton plied its waters. As in much of the South, Savannah's commerce and industry were ruled by "King Cotton" until Union blockade-runners closed the southern port in 1862. Savannah's most often-recounted Civil War tale, however, dates back to 1864 when Union general William Tecumseh Sherman spared the city as a Christmas present to President Abraham Lincoln.

Savannah's close proximity to a necklace of unspoiled barrier islands adds to your literary journey. Jekyll Island, St. Simon's Island, and Little St. Simon's Island are all within reach of Savannah.

The city enjoys an abundance of literary connections, from John Berendt's *Midnight in the Garden of Good and Evil* to Conrad Aiken and Flannery O'Connor, who spent their early childhood in the southern port. Scottish author Robert Louis Stevenson's name can also be added to a Savannah sojourn; he visited Savannah and immortalized it in his book *Treasure Island.*

The **Flannery O'Connor Childhood Home** is a recommended beginning. Located in the heart of the historic district near Lafayette Square, this Greek Revival town house is where Mary Flannery O'Connor was born in 1925. Managed and maintained by the Flannery O'Connor Childhood Home Foundation, the house is where the budding writer played as a child in the back-walled garden. Her family resided here until she was 12, when they moved to the Andalusia Farm in Milledgeville (see the "Milledgeville" section above). On display within the museum are vintage artifacts, mementos, photographs, and a selection of books belonging to the O'Connors. The fireplaces and chandeliers have been completely re-furbished and are reminiscent of the O'Connors' era.

Close by at 228 and 230 Oglethorpe Avenue is the **home of Conrad Aiken.** Near Forsyth Park, a Georgia Historical Marker denotes Aiken's residence. The house is privately owned, but a dramatic chapter in the writer's life took place here. Aiken, born in Savannah in 1889, suffered the tragic loss of his parents in February 1901 when his father shot his mother and then killed himself. Hearing gunshots, the youngster discov-ered his parents in the downstairs rooms and raced up the street to the police station to report the crime. After this harrowing and life-changing event, Aiken was sent to live with relatives in New England—only to re-turn to Savannah in 1962, when he lived next door to his boyhood home. His indelible memories of that fateful event never left him and influenced much of his writing.

Aiken's return to the city of his birth was a bittersweet and painful experience. He maintained a low profile while in residence and spent countless afternoons visiting his parents' grave site at **Bonaventure Ceme-tery.** Aiken is buried alongside them. His gravestone is in the shape of a bench and includes the inscription "Cosmos Mariner—Destination Un-known." Aiken's final wish was for his grave and that of his parents to be a place that visitors could frequent. Literary fans continue to visit the site, one of Bonaventure's most popular.

Midnight in the Garden of Good and Evil also begins in Bonaventure Ceme-tery. This is where *Bird Girl*, the sculpture that graced the cover of Berendt's bestselling book, was located until it was moved to the Telfair Museums. Berendt's affection for Savannah stemmed from many visits, eventually culminating in the creation of his novel. Berendt claimed that it was several books associated with Savannah that sparked his interest in the city, in-cluding Robert Louis Stevenson's *Treasure Island* and Margaret Mitchell's *Gone with the Wind*, where she described Savannah as "that gently managed city by the sea."

"Savannah," remarked Berendt on his website, "stood aloof on the Georgia coast—dignified, sedate, refined and looking its nose down at Atlanta. . . . These were the images in my mental gazetteer of Savannah, rum-drinking pirates, strong willed women, courtly manners, eccentric be-havior, gentle words and lovely music. . . . That and the beauty of the name itself, Savannah."

The Pirates' House, one of the oldest buildings in Georgia and today a popular dining spot, has a Robert Louis Stevenson association. Built in 1734, the building is where the Scottish author visited when in the United States. The house became a haven for pirates and sailors in the 1700s. There is a secret tunnel beneath the building that was used to shanghai sailors off to ships in the harbor. Hanging on the walls in the Captain's Room are pages and sketches from early editions of *Treasure Island.*

In the novel Captain Flint dies in the upstairs bedroom with Billy Bones at his side. On moonlit evenings the ghost of Captain Flint is rumored to wander along the hallway, adding to the building's myth and mystery.

Flannery O'Connor Childhood Home, 207 East Charlton Street, Savannah, GA 31401 (912-233-6014; www.flanneryoconnor home.org)

Bonaventure Cemetery, 330 Bonaventure Road, Savannah, GA 31404 (912-651-6843; www.bonaventurehistorical.org)

The Pirates' House, 20 East Broad Street, Savannah, GA 31401 (912-233-5757; www.thepirateshouse.com)

⚙ EXCURSIONS AND DIVERSIONS

SAVANNAH HIGHLIGHTS

Savannah offers a host of things to see and do, so plan on spending a few days in this captivating southern city. The **Mercer Mansion** is the central character in John Berendt's *Midnight in the Garden of Good and Evil* book and also happens to be one of the city's most treasured architectural landmarks. This is where the real-life story of Billy Hansen's murder—which figured in the novel's story line—took place. Designed by New York architect John S. Norris, the Mercer Mansion dates back to 1860 and is named after General Hugh W. Mercer, great-grandfather to musician Johnny Mercer of "Moon River" fame. The building was restored in 1969 by preservationist-historian Jim Williams, who filled the home with his private art collection. The Mercer Mansion is open to the public. The gift shop has a wide selection of *Midnight in the Garden of Good and Evil* souvenirs, including the book and replicas of the *Bird Girl* statue on its cover.

The **Telfair Museums** should also be on your list; this is where the the original *Bird Girl* statue is located. The museums make a great outing and include a café and bookstore.

When it comes to Savannah landmarks, **Mrs. Wilkes' Boarding House** on Jones Street is the place to go for genuine down-home southern cooking. A native of Savannah, Mrs. Sema Wilkes attracted diners with her fried chicken, butter beans, corn bread, and mashed potatoes served family-style from the day she opened her establishment in 1943. Customers have included newsman David Brinkley, who featured the spot on his nightly news show, and Walter Cronkite, who had dinner here before retiring from CBS News. Lines form early for the lunch-only eatery. Reporters continue to dine and cover this one-of-a-kind restaurant, certain to be a highlight on your literary Savannah tour.

Mercer Williams House Museum, 429 Bull Street, Monterey Square, Savannah, GA 31401 (912-236-6352; www.mercer house.com)

Telfair Museums, 121 Barnard Street, Atlanta, GA (912-790-8800; www.telfair.org)

Mrs. Wilkes' Boarding House, 107 West Jones Street, Savannah, GA 31401 (912-232-5997; http://mrswilkes.com)

⚘ LITERARY LODGING

THE SAVANNAH EXPERIENCE

Savannah has an abundance of historic inns and hotels. Two clear standouts are the Ballastone Inn and the Eliza Thompson House. Both establishments provide travelers with a thoroughly "Savannah experience."

The AAA Four-Diamond **Ballastone Inn,** billed as "Savannah's most romantic inn," is a perennial favorite. Constructed in 1838, the inn has 16 elegantly appointed guest rooms. Original art is displayed throughout the property, and a full southern breakfast and afternoon tea are included in your room rate. The **Eliza Thompson House,** dating back to 1847, was once the home of prominent Savannah residents Eliza and Joseph Thompson. Twelve rooms are in the main house, with a charming carriage house offering 13 rooms all distinctly designed and overlooking the courtyard. The courtyard features an original fountain by Ivan Bailey, one of Savannah's most prominent artists. A full southern breakfast is served there every morning.

Ballastone Inn, 14 East Oglethorpe Avenue, Savannah, GA 31401 (912-236-1484; www.ballastone.com)

Eliza Thompson House, 5 West Jones Street, Savannah, GA 31401 (912-236-3620; www.elizathompsonhouse.com)

GEORGIA'S GOLDEN ISLES

Some 90 miles from Savannah, the Golden Isles in Glynn County begin with the mainland port city of Brunswick and include a group of barrier islands off Georgia's Atlantic coast. The region provides the setting for Sidney Lanier's evocative poem "The Marshes of Glynn." Live oaks, Spanish moss, salt marshes, and a variety of wildlife make this one of Georgia's loveliest locales.

The state owns and operates the **Jekyll Island Club Hotel,** a historic landmark that from 1886 to 1942 was a winter getaway for the Astors, Rockefellers, Morgans, and Vanderbilts. The Who's Who of New York society traveled to the area by private railroad car, staying in various houses found throughout the property, with the main hotel the place to dine and dance. The 157-guest Victorian hotel is one of Georgia's best-kept secrets.

Twelve miles from Brunswick, this national treasure is listed on the National Register of Historic Places as well as being a part of the National Trust's Historic Hotels group. Restored to its former glory in 1986, the hotel features leaded art glass, ornate woodwork, Rumford fireplaces, verandas, and a lofty tower. Many scenes from Robert Redford's 2000 movie *The Legend of Bagger Vance* were filmed in the hotel's stately dining room. A private beach club, marina, croquet, charter fishing, carriage rides, and kayaking all provide pleasure here.

Jekyll Island Club Hotel, 371 Riverview Drive, Jekyll Island, GA 31527 (855-535-9547; www.jekyllclub.com)

ᒧ Sea Island

> *We went down to the Georgia coast, to the sea islands. We stayed at Sea
> Island Beach, a part of St. Simon's Island and it was heavenly quiet.
> There is no place in the world so still. No one knew us, the phone didn't
> ring and we rode through long avenues of enormous trees with yards of
> Spanish moss.*
>
> —THE LETTERS OF MARGARET MITCHELL

SEA ISLAND—Georgia's lush barrier island with its ethereal and mystical atmosphere—was a safe harbor and hideaway for Eugene O'Neill (*The Iceman Cometh*) and Margaret Mitchell (*Gone with the Wind*).

Largely uninhabited until 1928 when auto magnate Howard Coffin built a hotel here, the secluded resort became a welcome refuge for O'Neill, who traveled here to escape his literary fame. O'Neill and his wife, Carlotta, lived for a month at the **Cloister Hotel** before building their Spanish Mediterranean home, Casa Genotta. The secluded and serene setting along with its balmy climate appealed to the playwright, who enjoyed fishing and swimming when not writing.

O'Neill, who at age 25 wrote, "I want to be an artist or nothing," was born into a theatrical family. A large part of his childhood was spent being shuttled from one hotel to another. He looked upon Casa Genotta as his private creative sanctuary, moving into the house on June 22, 1932.

You'll find Casa Genotta—now known as Cottage 57—located off a winding road and a few miles from the Cloister Hotel. Constructed at a cost of $50,000, the house is available for rentals with a four-night minimum stay; it accommodates up to 12 guests. It has a swimming pool and has been styled to reflect what the O'Neills envisioned. The Spanish-style hacienda, designed by architect Francis Louis Abreau, has an upstairs study modeled after a ship's galleon and displays the desk where O'Neill wrote *Ah, Wilderness!*—"the play," he said, "which showed the way I would have liked my boyhood to have been." The upstairs study also has several volumes of O'Neill's work on the bookshelves, with the downstairs Grand Room being where here he did most of his editing in the evening.

Like fellow writers Ernest Hemingway and Zane Grey, O'Neill loved fishing and spent countless afternoons casting a line or sailing around the islands following his demanding early-morning writing regimen. While living here the couple entertained many literary friends, including Somerset Maugham and Sherwood Anderson. O'Neill's brief and happy interlude at Sea Island concluded in 1936. Seventeen years after his Sea Island odyssey, the playwright responsible for *Strange Interlude, The Iceman Cometh, Desire Under the Elms,* and *Long Day's Journey into Night* died in a New England hotel.

As quickly as the O'Neills departed the island, Margaret Mitchell arrived here following her enormous success with *Gone with the Wind.* Much like O'Neill, Mitchell came seeking privacy and seclusion. With newsmen camped out on her Atlanta doorstep monitoring her every move, Mitchell fled to the island, often registering under an assumed name. A native Georgian, she expounded on Sea Island's tranquility and wrote to a friend, "You won our hearts when you spoke glowingly of Savannah, for the stretch of coast from Savannah southward to Brunswick, is, to us, the most beautiful place in the world. . . . There is a pool to swim in, horses to ride, skeet shooting . . . but the nicest thing is to motor along the long sandy roads under the huge trees covered with moss. . . . There is a stillness of marsh water and trees like the day after creation, and this stillness never fails to have a soothing effect on this weary and harassed pair."

§ LITERARY LODGING

THE CLOISTER HOTEL

The Mobil Four-Star Cloister is modeled after an original 1928 building. Classified as a Mediterranean masterpiece, it has been rated as one of the Top 100 Resorts in the World by *Travel + Leisure* magazine. Guests can stay in the main building, the beach club, or private cottages—including **Cottage 57,** Eugene O'Neill's former home, Casa Genotta. The **Georgian Room** in the main building is Georgia's only Forbes Five-Star restaurant, serving a selection of seafood, steaks, and "Refined Southern Cuisine." Outings can be arranged for guests including sailing, kayaking, golf, tennis, and spa facilities.

The Cloister, Sea Island, 100 Cloister Drive, Sea Island, GA (1-855-627-9525; www.seaisland.com)

CHAPTER
4

$\mathcal{K}$ENTUCKY

THE UNDULATING EMERALD VALLEYS of horse country, the thunder of thoroughbreds entering the home stretch at Churchill Downs, the frontier vision of Daniel Boone—these images are at the heart of Kentucky's identity.

The Bluegrass State, so named because the limestone-rich soil lends a bluish hue to spring growth, has produced more Kentucky Derby champions than any other. The Derby's clarion call attracts spectators and horse lovers from around the globe desiring to catch a glimpse of "the two most exciting minutes in racing history."

Steeped in southern gentility, Kentucky broke away from the Old Dominion to forge its own identity, reflecting a western ruggedness. "Within these natural boundaries is Kentucky," wrote author Jesse Stuart in the poem "Kentucky Is My Land": "Shaped like the mouldboard on a hillside turning-plow. / Kentucky is neither southern, northern, eastern, nor western, / It is the core of America. / If these United States could be called a body, / Kentucky can be called its heart."

Kentucky holds the distinction of being the home state of Robert Penn Warren, the nation's first poet laureate, who was awarded the Pulitzer Prize for both poetry and fiction. Warren remains the state's most revered and celebrated author and is joined by fellow Kentucky scribes Allen Tate and Cleanth Brooks, members of the Fugitives, a group of poets and intellectuals centered on Nashville's Vanderbilt University. Warren's boyhood home in Guthrie has been faithfully preserved and is one of the most important stops on a Kentucky literary tour.

Louisville figures in F. Scott Fitzgerald's *The Great Gatsby*, and Lexington's William Wells Brown was the first African American novelist to be published. John Fox Jr., who wrote *Trail of the Lonesome Pine*, and the novelist and short-story writer James Lane Allen add to the state's literary talent. Theodore O Hara, author of the famous 19th-century poem "The Bivouac of the Dead," is interred in Frankfort.

THE ROBERT PENN WARREN LIBRARY, BOWLING GREEN

Western Kentucky University is home to the Robert Penn Warren Library. Warren's family donated his personal library to the university after his death. His widow, Eleanor Clark, wanted scholars as well as individuals interested in his literary career to have access to the items. Within the collection you'll find the laurel wreath given to him when he became poet laureate, first editions of his works, periodicals, personal correspondence, photographs, Warren's desk, and various memorabilia.

Western Kentucky University, 1906 College Heights Boulevard, Bowling Green, KY 42101 (270-745-0111; www.wku.edu/library)

ᴄ⁓ Frankfort

On Fame's eternal camping-ground
Their silent tents are spread,
And glory guards, with solemn round
The bivouac of the dead.
                —THEODORE O'HARA, "THE BIVOUAC OF THE DEAD"

PERCHED ON A HILLTOP overlooking the Kentucky Capitol is the final resting place of poet/journalist Theodore O'Hara. Situated on a bluff facing the Kentucky River, the **Frankfort Cemetery,** minutes from the capitol and governor's mansion, is also where Daniel Boone is interred.

O'Hara, born in Danville, Kentucky, became a journalist while serving as a volunteer in the Mexican-American War. His most recited poem, "The

Bivouac of the Dead," was penned in 1847 to honor Kentuckians who served and died in that war. Lines from the poem are found on his tombstone, as well as on many monuments throughout the South. The gateway to Arlington National Cemetery also features an inscription from the famous poem.

In November, Frankfort hosts the annual **Kentucky Book Fair** where over 100 nationally and internationally known authors are on hand to sign books and give readings.

Frankfort Cemetery, 215 East Main Street, Frankfort, KY 40601 (502-227-2403)

Kentucky Book Fair, PO Box 715, Frankfort, KY 40602 (502-229-2542; www.kybookfair.blogspot.com)

ᦂ Guthrie

What voice at moth-hour did I hear calling
As I stood in the orchard while the white
Petals of apple blossoms were falling,
Whiter than a moth wing in twilight?

—ROBERT PENN WARREN,
"WHAT VOICE AT MOTH-HOUR"

ROBERT PENN WARREN, c. 1968

AMERICA'S FIRST POET LAUREATE, Robert Penn Warren, was born in this small Kentucky community near the Tennessee border in 1905. Its leafy avenues and small-town atmosphere nurtured his early creative life. His parents, Franklin and Ruth Warren, filled their home with books. An avid reader from a young age, Warren was influenced by his Kentucky surroundings. His grandfather was also a major force in his childhood, taking him on adventurous outings as well as spending hours reading to him and telling him inspiring stories.

His birthplace, identified as a "railroad bungalow," is typical of middle-class dwellings at the turn of the 20th century. Now a permanent memorial to the writer, the redbrick house has been meticulously restored to depict Warren's early years, with period antiques, burnished hardwood floors, and family photographs scattered throughout. The house also serves as a research facility open to scholars, displaying a complete collection of Warren's works.

ROBERT PENN WARREN BIRTHPLACE MUSEUM
Courtesy of the Robert Penn Warren Birthplace Museum

Robert Penn Warren Birthplace Museum, 3rd and Cherry Streets, Guthrie, KY 42234 (270-483-2683; www.robert pennwarren.com)

ᴄ᷎ Lexington

> *The longer I live here, the better satisfied I am in having pitched my earthly camp-fire, gypsylike, on the edge of a town, keeping it on one side, and the green fields, lanes, and woods on the other. Each, in turn, is to me as a magnet to the needle. At times the needle of my nature points towards the country. . . . At others the needle veers round, and I go to town—to the massed haunts of the highest animal and cannibal.*
>
> —JAMES LANE ALLEN, *A Kentucky Cardinal*

A TRIO OF NAMES—James Lane Allen, John Fox Jr., and William Wells Brown—distinguish Lexington for the literary traveler. All of these writers were born in Lexington, whose historic district is abundant with restored Federal architecture. The city's Transylvania University was the alma mater of both Allen and Fox, who were classmates and lifelong friends.

Gratz Park is the location of James Lane Allen's gift to the citizens of Lexington, the *Fountain of Youth*, also referred to as the **James Lane Allen Fountain,** a bronze sculpture of a boy and a girl playing in a fountain pool. A plaque on the site commemorates Allen's Lexington roots. During Allen's lifetime he incorporated many Kentucky themes into his writings, as well as native Kentucky dialect, with some of his most popular works including *A Kentucky Cardinal* (1895) and *The Choir Invisible* (1898). Both of these books were bestsellers when published. **The Lexington Cemetery** is the final stop on the Allen excursion and where Allen is interred.

John Fox Jr., author of *Trail of the Lonesome Pine* and *The Little Shepherd of Kingdom Come*, was, in the words of one scholar, "a regional writer who painted a faithful and moving portrait of life in the southern mountains." Fox left Lexington to study at Harvard University and settled in Big Stone Gap, Virginia, where his home is open to the public (see the Virginia chapter).

William Wells Brown, thought to have been born on a plantation in Lexington, is believed to be America's first published African American novelist. His 1847 memoir, *Narrative of William Wells Brown, A Fugitive Slave* was followed in 1853 by the novel *Clotel; the President's Daughter; A Narrative of Slave Life in the United States.* Brown worked on a Lake Erie steamer and helped many black fugitives escape to freedom. He befriended French author Victor Hugo on a tour of Europe, where he lectured on the course of freedom.

Gratz Park Historic District (www.gratzpark.org or www.nps .gov/nr/travel/lexington/gra.htm)

Lexington Cemetery, 833 West Main Street, Lexington, KY 40508 (859-255-5522; www.lexcem.org)

§ LITERARY LODGING

THE GRATZ PARK INN

Named after Lexington businessman Benjamin Gratz, this inn is located in the heart of Lexington's historic district. Two blocks from Main Street, it is near antiques shops and home to one of Lexington's finest dining spots, **Jonathan.** It is also near the Lexington Opera House and Transylvania University. Its 41 rooms reflect a luxurious horsey theme; fine furnishings include four-poster beds.

Gratz Park Inn, 120 West Second Street, Lexington, KY 40507 (859-231-1777; www.gratzparkinn.com)

✿ EXCURSIONS & DIVERSIONS

TRAVELING THROUGH HORSE COUNTRY

Springtime is the best time of year to visit Lexington. The rolling meadows are alive with young foals. Kentucky's love affair with the horse is displayed at two outstanding Lexington sites that offer unbeatable glimpses into all things equine. The history, training, breeding, and racing of these magnificent animals comes alive at both sites.

The Kentucky Horse Park, covering more than 1,000 acres, is a day's outing in itself. Museums, barns, a picnic area, and a schedule of special events staged throughout the year make this stop a great choice for traveling families. More than 32 miles of white plank fencing, a Lexington trademark, gracefully outline the park's perimeter across the rambling Kentucky countryside.

The park pays homage to the horse and our relationship with this animal through exhibits, films, and several outlying barns that display over 25 breeds, from the Morgan to the quarter horse to the Clydesdale. A striking bronze sculpture of the legendary racehorse Man O'War greets visitors to the park's entrance. A gleaming state-of-the-art visitors center includes a gift shop.

At the park's International Museum of the Horse, visitors can explore a rich collection of 19th-century horse-drawn carriages and racing harnesses. Also within this area is the *Horse in Sport and Recreation* gallery, an exhibit that showcases Lexington's Calumet Farm. Gold and silver trophies and more than 35 paintings detailing images of Lexington's most famous horse farm, along with pictures of some of its winning thoroughbreds, are displayed here.

Keeneland, listed on the National Register of Historic Places, opened to the public in 1936. Some of the world's most famous trainers and jockeys have worked out at this beautiful track. Many of the scenes from the movie *Seabiscuit* were filmed at Keeneland, including the pivotal race between War Admiral and Seabiscuit.

The Track Kitchen is a must on a visit to Keeneland; early in the morning you can mingle with the jockeys and trainers and enjoy a hearty breakfast of scrambled eggs, Virginia ham, and homemade biscuits, served cafeteria-style.

Kentucky Horse Park, 4089 Iron Works Parkway, Lexington, KY 40511 (1-800-678-8813; www.kyhorsepark.com)

Keeneland, 4201 Versailles Road, Lexington, KY 40510 (859-254-3412; www.keeneland.com)

ᴄᴠ Louisville

> *In June she married Tom Buchanan of Chicago with more pomp and circumstance than Louisville ever knew before. He came down with a hundred people in four private cars and hired a whole floor of the Seelbach Hotel, and the day before the wedding he gave her a string of pearls valued at three hundred and fifty thousand dollars.*
>
> —F. Scott Fitzgerald, *The Great Gatsby*

F. SCOTT FITZGERALD
Courtesy of the Scott and Zelda Fitzgerald Museum

IN 1918, with the nation in the throes of the Great War, Scott Fitzgerald arrived in Louisville to begin his military training at Camp Taylor. He viewed the war in Europe as an adventure to enrich his life, both personally and creatively. It was his first trip south, and the southern way of life impressed him greatly. Daisy Fay, the heroine of his most famous novel, *The Great Gatsby*, hails from Louisville, and some of the book's most critical events take place in or around the city. From Kentucky, Fitzgerald would travel to Camp Sheridan in Montgomery, Alabama, where he met Zelda Sayre. (See chapter 1 for Fitzgerald sites in Montgomery.) Daisy Buchanan was largely modeled on Zelda and her southern-belle ways.

Kentucky's largest city, Louisville has several significant Fitzgerald connections. Lieutenant Scott Fitzgerald spent a month here, and it would prove to be a pivotal point in his literary career. He'd just completed the first draft of *The Romantic Egotist.* Having dropped out of Princeton and waiting for his first novel to be published, he viewed going off to the war in Europe as an exciting journey.

There are three major landmarks in Louisville associated with Fitzgerald and *The Great Gatsby*—the Seelbach Hotel, Cherokee Park, and Camp Taylor. The **Seelbach Hotel** proved most enthralling to the young author. When he was on leave from Camp Taylor, Fitzgerald enjoyed toasting his fellow officers in the **Rathskeller Lounge,** which was the headquarters for the USO in Louisville. The German-influenced vintage Rookwood pottery found there today is almost identical to what the writer must have seen.

On Fitzgerald's visits he often wandered the hotel's hallways, where he discovered the **Grand Ballroom** that was mentioned in *Gatsby* as the setting for Daisy Fay and Tom Buchanan's wedding. Today this elegant ballroom evokes the Fitzgerald spirit and era with its gold-and-cobalt décor, crystal chandeliers, and Palladian windows. This gorgeous room with a view mesmerized the writer.

THE SEELBACH HOTEL GRAND BALLROOM
Courtesy of The Seelbach Hilton, Louisville

A few miles from the Seelbach is **Cherokee Park,** an exclusive neighborhood then and now where one address, 2427 Cherokee Park, may have been the model for Daisy's house. (It's now privately owned and not open to the public.) The sprawling white-columned beauty with its expansive lawn seems right out of a Fitzgerald novel. In 1918—according to several local historians and scholars—many residents of this upscale neighborhood invited officers from Camp Taylor to social events. It's easy to envision the strapping Lieutenant Fitzgerald in his pressed uniform striding up the steps to attend a social event.

In *The Great Gatsby*, the character Jordan Baker remarks, "The largest of the banners and the largest of the lawns belonged to Daisy Fay's house. She was just eighteen, two years older than me, and by far the most popular of all the young girls in Louisville. She dressed in white, and had a little white roadster, and all day long the telephone rang in her house and excited young officers from Camp Taylor demanded the privilege of monopolizing her that night. 'Anyways, for an hour!'"

Camp Taylor no longer exists. Named after Zachary Taylor, it was located several miles from downtown. In Fitzgerald's day it was a training camp for over 125,000 troops. Constructed in 90 days, it was closed in 1920 at the end of World War I. Today a historical marker on the site mentions Camp Taylor.

When Gatsby's dream falters, Fitzgerald brings him back to Louisville following his tour of duty in Europe to reminisce about the romance that had played out on its impressive stage. "He came back from France," Fitzgerald wrote, "when Tom and Daisy were still on their wedding trip, and made a miserable but irresistible journey to Louisville on the last of his army pay. He stayed there a week, walking the streets where their footsteps had clicked together through the November night and revisiting the out-of-the-way places to which they had driven in her white car. Just as Daisy's house had always seemed to him more mysterious and gay than other houses, so his idea of the city itself, even though she was gone from it, was pervaded with a melancholy beauty."

And when Gatsby departs Louisville for the very last time and waits for the train that first carried him to the city, the memory of Daisy surfaces again in his writing. "The track curved and now it was going away from the sun, which, as it sank lower, seemed to spread itself in benediction over the vanishing city where she had drawn her breath. He stretched out his hand desperately as if to snatch only a wisp of air, to save a fragment of the spot that she had made lovely for him. But it was all going by too fast now for his blurred eyes and he knew that he had lost that part of it, the freshest and the best, forever."

THE SEELBACH HOTEL LOBBY
Courtesy of The Seelbach Hilton, Louisville

🕭 LITERARY LODGING

THE SEELBACH HILTON HOTEL

From the moment you step inside this grand southern hotel, you can easily imagine Tom and Daisy Buchanan slipping out of the pages of F. Scott Fitzgerald's masterpiece and gliding into the luxurious lobby. You know you have arrived when you stay in this AAA Four-Diamond facility.

This is a prime Fitzgerald haunt. Although the writer never overnighted at the hotel, at least not that we know of, he was certainly drawn to it, and his romantic sensibilities are reflected in Louisville's most historic and elegant property. Seven U.S. presidents have walked through its portals, as did the notorious gangster Al Capone. Listed on the National Register of Historic Places, the Beaux-Arts baroque hotel was founded in 1905 by Otto and Louis Seelbach. A $12 million renovation is evident everywhere from the bronzes from France to the hardwoods from the West Indies and the linens from Ireland. No expense has been spared to make this the city's most luxurious lodging.

THE FITZGERALD SUITE
Courtesy of The Seelbach Hilton, Louisville

The hotel's literary connections are celebrated in the Fitzgerald Suite, which offers a parlor, dining area, two bedrooms, and three bathrooms. The Gatsby Suite takes luxury to a whole new level offering a parlor, foyer, three bedrooms, and four bathrooms. The **Oakroom** has the largest wine cellar in the region and is Kentucky's only AAA Five-Diamond restaurant.

Seelbach Hilton Louisville, 500 South 4th Street, Louisville, KY 40202 (502-585-3200; www.seelbachhilton.com)

⊕ **EXCURSIONS & DIVERSIONS**

EXPLORING LOUISVILLE

No trip to Louisville is complete without a stop at **Churchill Downs,** whose twin spires frame the most famous racetrack in the world. Tours are available. The **Kentucky Derby Museum** is a site that will entertain you for hours. A movie titled *The Greatest Race* on a 360-degree screen captures all of the drama, beauty, and excitement of thoroughbred racing. Exhibits, photographs, and the history of this amazing race come alive at this vintage American landmark. To experience the Ohio River, board the *Belle of Louisville* and the *Spirit of Jefferson* in the spring; dining is offered on the excursion.

Kentucky is of course home to some of the best bourbon in the world. Cap off your visit to this part of the world by following the **Bourbon Trail**—a dining and walking trail connecting the best bourbon-sippin' spots in downtown Louisville.

Churchill Downs, 700 Central Avenue, Louisville, KY 40214 (502-636-4400; www.churchilldowns.com)

Belle of Louisville, 401 West River Road, Louisville, KY 40202 (502-574-2992 or 1-866-832-0011; www.belleoflouisville.org)

Kentucky Bourbon Trail, 614 Shelby Street, Frankfort, KY 40601 (502-875-9351; http://kybourbontrail.com)

Louisville CVB, One Riverfront Plaza, 401 West Main Street, Suite 2300, Louisville, KY 40280 (502-584-2121, 1-800-626-5646, www.gotolouisville.com)

*L*OUISIANA

F EW STATES IN THE AMERICAN SOUTH evoke as much mystery and enchantment as Louisiana. Its spicy blend of Cajun and Creole customs, along with the rowdy merriment of Mardi Gras, its most famous festival, make it not only a magnet for creativity but also the South's most alluring destination. Mist-filled lagoons and bayous showcase its stunning geography. Snowy-white egrets hovering above alligator-infested swamps draped in Spanish moss add to its haunting beauty. Pirates once roamed these brackish waters.

The War of 1812, Andrew Jackson, pirate Jean Lafitte, and the Battle of New Orleans are just a few pages from the illustrious history of Louisiana, the 18th state to enter the Union. The River Road plantations just outside New Orleans personify its southern setting, with the meandering Mississippi adding to its appeal and history.

Names of the notable surface as you travel through the state. William Faulkner began his literary journey in New Orleans. Tennessee Williams wrote most of his most acclaimed works in the City That Care Forgot. Robert Penn Warren penned his Pulitzer Prize–winning novel *All the King's Men* while living and teaching at LSU in Baton Rouge.

An important writer associated with the Harlem Renaissance, Arna Bontemps, had Louisiana associations; so did Anne Rice, who sculpted her *Vampire Chronicles* while living in the New Orleans Garden District.

Walker Percy's *The Moviegoer,* John Kennedy Toole's *A Confederacy of Dunces,* and Lillian Hellman's *The Little Foxes* all tell stories about New Orleans.

Discovering Louisiana's abundance of literary sites and authors could prove to be your most fascinating excursion.

⌘ Alexandria

> *Let us keep the dance of rain our fathers kept and tread our dreams beneath the jungle sky.*
>
> —ARNA BONTEMPS

BORN IN 1902 TO CREOLE PARENTS, the poet Arna Bontemps is associated with the Harlem Renaissance. He is credited with writing over 20 books, and was a noted anthologist. His poetry is considered his greatest literary contribution, along with his 1931 novel, *God Sends Sunday.* The **Arna Bontemps African American Museum** is his birthplace; here exhibits devoted to his writings, life, and work celebrate his legacy. Photographs, letters, and family memorabilia are on display in the restored building, which is part of the **Louisiana African American Heritage Trail.** The museum also hosts special events such as "Jazz on the River," and a birthday symposium staged in September featuring readings, lectures, and seminars.

Bontemps taught at the Harlem Academy in New York in 1926, where he forged a lasting friendship with Langston Hughes, who became a major influence. Their creative collaboration included *Popo and Fifina* (1932), a children's book. Their correspondence is collected in *Arna Bontemps–Langston Hughes Letters, 1925–1967.*

Bontemps made a significant contribution in compiling black literature, and in 1943 he became the head librarian at Fisk University in Nashville, where he developed one of the most comprehensive archives of African American cultural materials, namely the Langston Hughes Renaissance Collection.

Arna Bontemps African American Museum, 1327 3rd Street, Alexandria, LA 71301 (318-473-4692; arnabontempsmuseum .com)

Louisiana African American Heritage Trail (www.astory
likenoother.com)

⌒ Baton Rouge

> *When I pulled into the Capitol grounds I saw that the place was pretty
> well lit up. But that wasn't surprising, even at that hour, when the Leg-
> islature was in session. And when I got inside, the place was certainly
> not uninhabited. The solons had broken up shop for the evening and were
> milling about in the corridors, especially at those strategic points where
> the big brass spittoons stood. There were a lot of reporters, and herds of
> bystanders, those people who love to have the feeling that they are around
> when something big is happening.*
>
> —ROBERT PENN WARREN, *All the King's Men*

HUEY LONG STATUE IN BATON ROUGE

AS YOU APPROACH LOUISIANA'S CAPITAL,
the towering statehouse looms over the city like
a phoenix reaching up into the sky. The 34-story
structure is the tallest state capitol in the country
and embodies former governor Huey Long's
dream. It was constructed at a cost of $5 million;
25 railcars were required to transport the limestone for its ornate interior. This is where Robert
Penn Warren became inspired to write *All the
King's Men,* the novel that became the signature
work of his literary career and won the Pulitzer
Prize in 1947.

Long, who transformed Baton Rouge and
Louisiana into a thriving economic force, was a
larger-than-life character who assumed the guise
of Willie Stark in Warren's compelling novel. The Kentucky writer arrived
at LSU at the request of Long, who desperately wanted to elevate the university's reputation in the arts and humanities. Warren, along with John
Crowe Ransom and Allen Tate, fellow Fugitive writers from Vanderbilt
University, was part of Long's grand and ambitious plan. He worked as
an assistant professor of English from 1933 until 1942 and admitted

following the book's enormous success that had he not gone to Louisiana, "the novel never would have been written."

He spent countless hours at the capitol and ripped pages from the headlines in mapping out the story of Willie Stark and Sugar Boy, the novel's two main characters. "Real writers are those who want to write, need to write, have to write," Warren said in an interview. His own writing exquisitely captured the essence of Long and the political climate of Depression-era Louisiana.

Touring the statehouse is a bit like leafing through pages of *All the King's Men* where Warren vividly describes the building, as well as Stark's rise to power and eventual demise. "We came out into the great lobby," he wrote, "under the dome, there was a blaze of light over the statues which stood with statesmanlike dignity on pedestals to mark the quarters of the place, and over the people who moved about in the area. We walked along the east wall, toward the inset where the elevators were. Just as we approached the statue of General Moffat (a great Indian fighter, a successful land speculator, the first governor of the state), I noticed a figure leaning against the pedestal."

Much like Stark in the novel, Long was assassinated while walking along one of the corridors in 1935. Warren was working on the book when Long was killed, adding to the book's dramatic conclusion. "Then I saw what was in his hand," he wrote, "and even as I recognized the object, but before the significance of the recognition had time to form itself in my mind and nerves, I saw the two little spurts of pale-orange flame from the muzzle of the weapon."

A capitol tour should definitely include the 25th-floor Observation Deck, which offers a panoramic view of Baton Rouge and the Mississippi River. You can also see the capitol grounds and gardens where Long's statue and grave are located.

Some additional Warren sites include the **Robert Penn Warren Room** in the Louisiana State University English Department, organized by Professor David Madden. Here a display of photographs and material pertaining to Warren's

LOUISIANA STATE CAPITOL BUILDING

LSU career can be studied. You can make arrangements to visit the site through the English Department. Another major literary association is found at the **T. Harry Williams Center for Oral History.** Williams, a renowned historian and author, wrote a biography of Huey Long that was awarded the Pulitzer Prize.

SOUTHERN REVIEW EDITORS ROBERT PENN WARREN, JAMES OLNEY, CLEANTH BROOKS, AND LEWIS P. SIMPSON   *Courtesy of Louisiana State University*

Every October LSU hosts the **Louisiana Book Festival,** attracting authors from around the country. It's held on the capitol grounds in front of the library. Special events, readings, and tours are offered on the weekend.

Louisiana State Capitol Building and Gardens, North 3rd Street on State Capitol Drive, Baton Rouge, LA 70802

Louisiana State University, Department of English, 260 Allen Hall, Baton Rouge, LA 70803 (225-578-4086; www.english.lsu .edu)

THE SOUTHERN REVIEW

It was while at Louisiana State University in 1936 that Robert Penn Warren cofounded *The Southern Review* with prominent literary critic Cleanth Brooks. Under their creative guidance the quarterly journal became one of the nation's most respected literary magazines, publishing the works of Katherine Anne Porter, Eudora Welty, Wallace Stevens, and T. S. Eliot. A plaque in LSU's Thomas Boyd Hall identifies the original offices of *The Southern Review.*

LITERARY LODGING

THE HILTON BATON ROUGE CAPITAL CENTER

On the National Register of Historic Places, the Hilton Baton Rouge Capital Center hotel dates back to 1927 and is adjacent to the Shaw Center for the Arts in downtown Baton Rouge. Every governor from 1928 until 1980 stayed at the hotel, including Huey

Long. Other former visitors include Robert Penn Warren, Will Rogers, and President John F. Kennedy. Its close proximity to both the capitol and LSU make the Hilton an ideal choice for seeing the area's highlights.

Hilton Baton Rouge Capitol Center, 201 Lafayette Street, Baton Rouge, LA 70801 (225-344-5866; www.3hilton.com)

⊕ EXCURSIONS AND DIVERSIONS

EXPLORING BATON ROUGE

Mark Twain once remarked that the **Old State Capitol Building** in Baton Rouge was the "ugliest building on the Mississippi River." You can see for yourself if you decide to tour the unusual building. Built in the Gothic style, it certainly stands out on a walk through Baton Rouge. During the Civil War the building served as a Union prison. In 1932 the current capitol assumed duties as statehouse. The Old State Capitol was turned into the Museum of Political History in 1994.

For cultural offerings near the LSU campus, the **Shaw Center for the Arts** includes art museums and galleries along with theater space where special events and concerts take place. Shops and cafés make this a delightful a break from your capitol touring.

Louisiana's Old State Capitol Museum of Political History, 100 North Boulevard, Baton Rouge, LA 70801 (225-342-0500 or 1-800-488-2968; www.louisianaoldstatecapitol.org)

Shaw Center for the Arts, 100 Lafayette Street, Baton Rouge, LA 70801 (225-346-5001; www.shawcenter.org)

Louisiana Book Festival, 701 N. Fourth Street, Baton Rouge, LA 70802 (225-219-9503, www.louisianabookfestival.org)

Visit Baton Rouge, 359 Third Street, Baton Rouge, LA 70801 (225-383-1825, 1-800-LaRouge, www.visitbatonrouge.com)

ᕲ New Orleans

*Don't you just love these long rainy afternoons in New Orleans when
an hour isn't just an hour—but a little bit of Eternity dropped in your
hands—and who knows what to do with it?*

—TENNESSEE WILLIAMS, *A Streetcar Named Desire*

AT TWILIGHT THE COBBLESTONES in
the French Quarter shimmer following an
afternoon rain. Streetlamps cast an amber
glow as you walk around the South's most
alluring and romantic destination. It's as if
time has stood still in the European-in-
fused port with its rainbow-colored architecture. "New Orleans," Stella comments
in Tennessee Williams's famous play, "isn't
like other cities."

Many literary luminaries have lingered
in the steamy, sultry port at the southernmost point of the Mississippi River. It's
easy to imagine Mark Twain—who immortalized the Mississippi in so many of
his stories—arriving by steamboat to wander the city.

TENNESSEE WILLIAMS
*Courtesy Library of Congress from New York World-Telegram & Sun
Collection. Photo by Orland Fernandez*

New Orleans perhaps more than any other city in the South has
proven a magnet for a host of writers. Anne Rice, John Kennedy Toole,
Walker Percy, and Lillian Hellman spring to mind. William Faulkner and
Sherwood Anderson also came to New Orleans seeking literary inspiration, as did Frances Parkinson Keyes, F. Scott Fitzgerald, Truman Capote,
and Eudora Welty.

But no writer is more closely associated with New Orleans than Tennessee Williams, who penned most of his most important works while
living here. *Summer and Smoke, The Rose Tattoo, Vieux Carré,* and *A Streetcar Named
Desire* all reveal his affection for—if not obsession with—the city. "If I
can be said to have a home," Williams wrote, "it is in New Orleans, where
I've lived off and on since 1938 and which has provided me with more
material than any other part of the country."

Born in Mississippi and raised in St. Louis, Williams arrived in New

Orleans in 1939 to escape an unhappy past. He once said that he came to the city "as a migratory bird going in search of a more congenial climate." In a letter to his mother, Williams wrote, "I'm crazy about the city. I walk continually, there is so much to see. The weather is balmy, today like early summer. . . . The [French] Quarter is really quainter than anything I've seen abroad—in many homes the original atmosphere is completely preserved." He worked at a succession of odd jobs by day to support himself while writing by night. The city's inherent artistic atmosphere provided Williams a wealth of material for his plays.

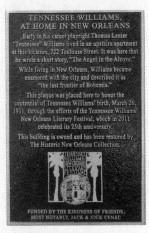

A BRONZE PLAQUE MARKS
WILLIAMS'S FIRST RESIDENCE AT
722 TOULOUSE STREET

Several key Williams landmarks are located in the French Quarter and marked with bronze plaques. His first residence was **722 Toulouse.** He was reputed to have written *A Streetcar Named Desire* at **632 St. Peters Street** after hearing "that rattletrap of a streetcar that bangs up one old street and down another." His final residence in New Orleans is found at **1014 Dumaine,** a pale pink stucco building where he lived from 1965 until his death in 1983. The Dumaine home was dedicated as a literary landmark in 2006 by the Friends of the New Orleans Public Library. All these sites are private; please respect the current tenants and enjoy seeing the exteriors and bronze plaques.

Williams was a committed writer throughout his career. "Writing for me," he said, "is a continual see-saw between rapture and despair which leaves me so exhausted, nervously and physically, that I actually believe each play reduces my life expectancy by several years."

When not working, Williams enjoyed and soaked up the exciting atmosphere of the French Quarter, often dining at his favorite restaurant, **Galatoire's,** where he requested the corner window table downstairs. All of the waiters knew his name and what cocktail he preferred to accompany his dinner. The historic **St. Louis Cathedral** that frames Jackson Square was another prime haunt for the playwright. A memorial service was held in the church following his death. Still, the largest tribute to the city's favorite writer is the five-day **Tennessee Williams Literary Festival,** where

TENNESSEE WILLIAMS
Courtesy Library of Congress from New York World-Telegram & Sun Collection. Photo by Walter Albertin.

readings, walking tours, seminars, and a "Stella"-shouting contest are staged to honor him—along with theatrical performances, of course.

Galatoire's, 209 Bourbon Street, New Orleans, LA 70130 (504-525-2021; www.galatoires.com)

Tennessee Williams/New Orleans Literary Festival, 938 Lafayette Street #514, New Orleans, LA 70113 (504-581-1144; www.tennesseewilliams.net)

⚙ EXCURSIONS AND DIVERSIONS

EXPLORING NEW ORLEANS

If you really want to see the city in the Williams spirit, then a streetcar ride on the **St. Charles Streetcar**— the oldest continuously running streetcar in the country—is a must. The Desire Line he immortalized has long since been retired, but you can board the historic green trolleys in the

ST. CHARLES STREETCAR

French Quarter and ride to the Garden District, where an array of antebellum architecture lines the streets. This will likely prove your most memorable jaunt in New Orleans.

A highly recommended dining spot and favorite for the college crowd is the **Camellia Grill,** a New Orleans landmark. The best pecan pie this side of the Mississippi and stacked-high burgers are worth the long lines on weekends. Pecan waffles are an added treat—not to mention the white-jacketed waiters, who know more about the city than most guides. Serving guests since 1946, this eatery will serve up a taste of genuine New Orleans.

St. Charles Streetcar, New Orleans Regional Transit Authority (504-248-3900; www.norta.com)

Camellia Grill, 626 South Carrollton Avenue, New Orleans, LA
70118 (504-309-2679)

The French Quarter

William Faulkner embraced New Orleans with as much passion as Tennessee Williams. The city was where he became inspired to write his first novel, *Soldiers' Pay.*

Arriving by train in 1925, Faulkner wrote for *The Double Dealer,* a literary journal based in the city, as well as the *New Orleans Times-Picayune* where he put together stories titled "New Orleans Sketches." He befriended Sherwood Anderson while living in New Orleans and subleased a ground-floor apartment at **624 Pirates Alley.** Faulkner's roommate was artist and architect William Spratling, with whom he collaborated on the book *Sherwood Anderson and Other Famous Creoles.* But Faulkner's time in the city was brief. It was Anderson who persuaded him to head home to Oxford and write about the region he knew and loved so much. In effect, the Yoknaptawpha stories began in New Orleans. He wrote of the city, "New Orleans: A courtesan, not old and yet no longer young, who shuns the sunlight that the illusion of her former glory be preserved. The mirrors in her house are dim and the frames are tarnished; all her house is dim and beautiful with age."

Faulkner's former address is now **Faulkner House Books,** an independent bookstore that specializes in rare books and works by major southern writers. Past book signing events have included William Styron, Willie Morris, Barry Hannah, and Roy Blount Jr. A plaque outside the building pays tribute to Faulkner. This is also where you can opt to take a literary walking tour with W. Kenneth Holditch, a resident scholar and literary fan. Each October the **Pirate's Alley Faulkner Society** pays tribute to Faulkner by hosting **Words & Music,** a five-day event that celebrates Faulkner's birthday with readings, events, and concerts.

Although the Faulkner House is open to the public, most of the French Quarter literary sites are privately owned, with the exception of the former home of Frances Parkinson Keyes, the **Beauregard-Keyes House,** located at 1113 Chartres Street and listed on the National Register of Historic Places. This is where the writer completed *Dinner at Antoine's* and *The Blue Camellia.* Keyes set up a foundation to ensure that the property would be protected as a historic landmark. On a more contemporary note, a life-sized bronze statue of Ignatius Reilly from John Kennedy Toole's *A Confederacy of Dunces* stands at **800 Iberville Street.**

> **Faulkner House Books,** 624 Pirate's Alley, New Orleans, LA 70119 (504-524-2940; www.faulkner house.net)
>
> **Beauregard-Keyes House,** 1113 Chartres Street, New Orleans, LA 70116 (504-523-7257; http://bkhouse.org)

BRONZE STATUE OF
IGNATIUS REILLY

The Garden District

Although the French Quarter with its wrought-iron balconies, lovely courtyards, and lazy tempo is abundant with literary associations, the Garden District, resplendent with its antebellum architecture and planters' cottages, boasts its own list of enviable literary talent.

Playwright Lillian Hellman was born in New Orleans as the only child of Max Hellman and Julia Newhouse. She grew up at **1718 Prytania,** one block off St. Charles, and patterned much of her play *The Little Foxes* after her mothers' affluent family. As a child she lived half the year in New York and the other half in New Orleans, where she spent considerable time with her grandmother, often dining at Tujaque's for lunch. Her former residence is privately owned.

In the 1920s F. Scott Fitzgerald lived briefly in a rooming house at **2900 Prytania.** He came to the city to escape the cold winters and was also concerned about tuberculosis. It was during his very brief stay in New Orleans that he traveled to Montgomery several times to visit Zelda Sayre and subsequently became engaged. While living here he completed the story "A Camel's Back." "It was written," he said in an interview, "during one day in the city of New Orleans with the express purpose of buying a platinum and diamond wrist watch which cost six hundred dollars. I began it at seven in the morning and finished it at two o'clock the same night."

Walker Percy is another name associated with the Garden District. The Mississippi writer taught at Loyola University in the 1970s, basing much of *The Moviegoer* on postwar New Orleans. Reminders of his legacy are found at Loyola's **Walker Percy Center for Writing and Publishing** and its Monroe Library, to which he bequeathed many of his letters, works, and photographs. In 2011 a literary weekend named in his honor was initiated. Percy is interred at **St. Joseph's Abbey** in nearby Covington, where he resided most of his life.

In an interview Percy elaborated on his love of movies and *The Moviegoer.* "It wasn't escapist," he said, "I was getting to know how people looked at the world and what they thought." Percy's path to becoming a writer was by happenstance. Following his studies at the University of North Carolina–Chapel Hill he contracted tuberculosis, cutting his medical career short. "I was the happiest doctor who ever got tuberculosis and was able to quit. It gave me an excuse to do what I wanted to do."

George Washington Cable's former home is found at **1313 8th Street.** The novelist was known for his depiction of Creole life in the city. The residence is listed on the National Register of Historic Places. Cable lived in the house from 1874 to 1884.

Former New Orleans resident Anne Rice penned the *Vampire Chronicles* series. In one interview Rice expounded on the hypnotic effect of New Orleans and how it has influenced her novels. "It's tropical and humid and decadent," she said, "and because of the incredible laziness here, it is filled with some of the most beautiful architecture in the United States— because nobody has bothered to tear it down. It's because we are a depressed city, a poor city, that all of the wonderful old houses have not been torn down. They are still standing, and the people here have come to love and value them." A key Rice site is the **Lafayette Cemetery No. 1,** in the 1400 block of Washington Avenue, where her fictional Mayfair witches were interred and where she has appeared for many promotional events.

Walker Percy Center for Writing and Publishing, 6363 St. Charles Avenue, New Orleans, LA 70118 (504-864-7041; www.loyno.edu/wpc)

Lafayette Cemetery No. 1, 1400 Washington Avenue, New Orleans, LA 70130 (504-525-3377)

⚜ LITERARY LODGING

THE HOTEL MONTELEONE

Hotel Monteleone is *the* New Orleans literary hotel. A long list of noted writers has either stayed at, visited, or been associated with this lovely property, which is ideally located in the heart of the

French Quarter. Designated as National Literary Landmark by the American Library Association, the Monteleone dates back to 1886.

William Faulkner stayed here in 1929 on his honeymoon with Estelle Oldham and again in 1951 when he was the recipient of the French Legion of Honor. According to Faulkner biographers, as much as he loved the Peabody in Memphis, the Monteleone was his favorite hotel. Truman Capote also has an important connection here: Hotel staff assisted his mother in getting to a hospital prior to his birth. Eudora Welty mentions the hotel in her short story "The Purple Hat." Tennessee Williams first visited the hotel with his grandfather Walter Dakin and wrote about it in his play *The Rose Tattoo.* Ernest Hemingway mentions the Monteleone in his short story "Night Before Battle." More recent literary guests have included Winston Groom and Richard Ford. The AAA Four-Star hotel has literary suites named in honor of William Faulkner, Ernest Hemingway, Eudora Welty, Tennessee Williams, and Truman Capote.

Hotel Monteleone, 214 Royal Street, New Orleans, LA 70130 (504-523-3341; www.hotelmonteleone.com)

⚜ EXCURSIONS AND DIVERSIONS

EXPLORING NEW ORLEANS

New Orleans offers a host of things to see and do whether your interest be literarature, music, architecture, or nature. Following your literary walking tour—offered through **Historic Tours of New Orleans** and the Faulkner House—you can opt to explore the **Audubon Zoo** in the Garden District or take any number of day trips from the city.

You might also spend some time savoring the southern architecture along the **Great River Road,** 50 miles east of New Orleans. Mark Twain traveled this route on his visit to the city. Houmas House, Oak Alley, and Destrehan and Nottoway Plantations are just a sampling of treasures you can discover on this easy and highly recommended day trip. Or simply enjoy the music and food this city is famous for; there's always something exciting to do in New Orleans.

New Orleans Tour Center, 612 Pelican Street, New Orleans, LA 70114; 504-533-4544 www.neworleanstourcenter.org

New Orleans CVB, 2020 St. Charles Avenue, New Orleans, LA 70130, 504-566-5011; www.neworleanscvb.com

Audubon Nature Institute, 6500 Magazine Street, New Orleans, LA 70118, 1-800-774-7394; www.auduboninstitute.org

ℳISSISSIPPI

O F ALL THE SOUTHERN STATES, Mississippi has produced perhaps the richest repository of major American authors. In Oxford, Faulkner created his fictional Yoknapatawpha County. Columbus was the birthplace of dramatist Tennessee Williams. Eudora Welty played as child and listened to countless stories from her parents in Jackson, the state capital. Shelby Foote and Walker Percy are connected here as well, along with Richard Ford, Margaret Walker Alexander, and Richard Wright. Even today, Mississippi continues to nurture new and burgeoning talent.

Old South traditions run deep in the state, which of course takes its name from the river that flows along its western border. The Mississippi Delta was the birthplace of the Delta blues. The area was prime cotton-growing territory in the 19th century, and Mississippi is home to an impressive collection of historic properties, most notably in Natchez, with its southern mansions in the Greek Revival style. An Ole Miss football game against rival Alabama on an autumn afternoon ranks high on Mississippi's events calendar.

What is it about this state that has produced such a wellspring of literary talent? The quiet southern towns, the magnolias along the riverfront, the echoes of the Confederate war dead are but a few of the elements that have engaged the creative energies of the writers who have found inspiration here.

In Mississippi, storytelling is a way of life.

THE GRISHAM ROOM

Learn more about bestselling author John Grisham's writing career at Mississippi State University, where the Grisham Room, dedicated in 1998, pays tribute to its most famous graduate. The exhibit is on the third floor of the Mitchell Memorial Library. The original manuscript of *A Time to Kill*, correspondence, photographs and translations of his novels are part of the collection.

John Grisham Room, Mitchell Memorial Library, MSU, 395 Hardy Road, Mississippi State, MS 39762 (662-325-6634; http://library .msstate.edu/grishamroom)

ᐺ Clarksdale

Home is where you hang your childhood.

—Tennessee Williams

THE MISSISSIPPI DELTA provided the backdrop for Tennessee Williams's early childhood. Born in Columbus, Williams and his mother and sister moved with his grandfather, Walter Dakin, an Episcopal priest, to Clarksdale at the age of three, while Williams's father traveled on business.

Dakin was rector at **St. George's Episcopal Church;** the family lived in the parsonage there. It is believed that this small southern town provided material for many of Williams's most important works, including *Cat on a Hot Tin Roof,* in which Big Daddy describes the Delta as "the richest land this side of the valley Nile." Williams was intrigued by the goings-on at the lavish **Cutrer Mansion** at 109 Clark Street. He visited this Italian Renaissance villa when he accompanied his grandfather on parish calls. The mansion is thought to be the model for *A Streetcar Named Desire's* Belle Reve. Today it is the **Cutrer Cultural Arts Center,** part of the Coahoma County Higher Education Center. **The Tennessee Williams Park** is named after the playwright.

Clarksdale CVB, 1540 DeSoto Avenue, Clarksdale, MS 38614 (662-627-7337; www.clarksdale.com/chamber)

St. George's Episcopal Church, 106 Sharkey Street, Clarksdale, MS (662-627-7875; www.stgeorges.dioms.org)

Cutrer Cultural Center for the Arts, 109 Clark Street, Clarksdale, MS 38614

🖋 LITERARY LODGING

CLARK HOUSE

Sixty miles from Oxford and 75 miles from Memphis is the Clark House. Several rooms in this historic district inn have Williams associations and names: Big Daddy, Stella, and Desire. Clark House dates back to 1859 and during the annual Tennessee Williams Festival hosts porch plays with the audience sitting in lawn chairs. A southern-style home offering eight rooms and a continental breakfast, Clark House is next door to the Cutrer Mansion where Williams made parish calls with his grandfather. It is believed to be the model for "Belle Reve," the former home of Blanche and Stella.

Clark House, 211 Clark Street, Clarksdale, MS 38614 (662-621-1632; www.clarkhouse.info)

ᴄ᷎ᴠ Columbus

> *I shall really have to go back South pretty soon and renew my acquaintance with some of our old home-towns such as Columbus if I am going to continue to write about them.*
>
> —TENNESSEE WILLIAMS,
> LETTER TO WALTER DAKIN, SEPTEMBER 9, 1946

TENNESSEE WILLIAMS WAS BORN in Columbus in 1911, and baptized by his grandfather, the Reverend Walter Dakin, at **St. Paul's Episcopal Church,** a key Williams site in this area. Once the rectory for St. Paul's, the Victorian house was relocated for preservation purposes in 1993; it was designated a National Literary Landmark and is now the **Tennessee**

Williams Welcome Center. The family lived in the home until moving to Clarksdale.

> **St. Paul's Episcopal Church,** 318 College Street, Columbus, MS (662-328-6673; www.stpaulscolumbus.dioms.org)
>
> **Tennessee Williams Welcome Center,** 300 Main Street, Columbus MS 39701 (662-328-0222)

EUDORA WELTY'S "WORLD TO ITSELF"

Arriving in Columbus from Jackson, Mississippi, in 1925 to attend the Mississippi University for Women was one Eudora Welty, who memorably describes the experience in her memoir *One Writer's Beginnings:* "There I landed in a world to itself, and indeed it was all new to me. It was surging with twelve hundred girls. They came from every nook and corner of the state, from the Delta, the piney woods, the Gulf Coast, the black prairie, the red clay hills." Welty attended the school until 1927. MUW, or The W, as it is known (now coeducational), commemorates its famous alumna with **Welty Drive** and an annual **Eudora Welty Writers' Symposium.**

Mississippi University for Women, 1100 South 2nd Avenue, Columbus, MS 39701 (662-329-4750; www.muw.edu)

ᖇ Greenville

> My country is the Mississippi Delta, the river country. It lies flat, like a badly drawn half oval, with Memphis at its northern and Vicksburg at its southern tip. Its western boundary is the Mississippi River, which coils and returns on itself in great loops and crescents. . . . With us when you speak of "the river," though there be many, you mean always the same one, the great river, the shifting, unappeasable god of the country, feared and loved, the Mississippi.
>
> —WILLIAM ALEXANDER PERCY, *Lanterns on the Levee*

GREENVILLE, WHICH LIES in the heart of the Mississippi Delta, has been called the "Athens of the Delta"—more than 60 writers have stoked their imaginations from its low-lying landscape, with Walker Percy and Shelby Foote the most renowned.

Following the tragic deaths of Walker Percy's parents—his father by suicide and his mother in a car accident two years later—he and his two brothers were adopted by a cousin, "Uncle Will" (William Alexander Percy). A bachelor lawyer, Uncle Will was the single most important influence in Walker's life. Walker elaborated on his cousin's generosity in one interview: "I will say no more than he was the most extraordinary man I have ever known and that I owe him a debt which cannot be repaid."

It was through Uncle Will that Walker first met Shelby Foote when the two future writers were still youths. They became lifelong friends, sharing their love of books and travel. Both attended the University of North Carolina–Chapel Hill. In one daring escapade, the two men set out for Oxford to meet their literary idol, William Faulkner. But while Foote had no trouble walking up to the front door and introducing himself, Percy stayed behind in the car.

Greensville has paid tribute to all of these men at several sites. The **William Alexander Percy Memorial Library** holds a collection of Uncle Will's writings. There is a Mississippi Historical Marker in Greenville's downtown area displaying the names of Foote, Walker Percy, William Alexander Percy, Charles Bell, Bern Keating, Ellen Douglas, David Cohn, and Hodding Carter Jr.

William Alexander Percy Memorial Library, 341 Main Street, Greenville, MS 38701 (662-335-2331; www.washington.lib.ms .us/percylibrary.htm)

✿ EXCURSIONS AND DIVERSIONS

THE MISSISSIPPI DELTA CULTURAL TOUR
Annually the Mississippi Delta Cultural Tour offers an in-depth literary tour of the region, exploring its literature, food, and culture. Organized by the Center for the Study of Southern Culture in Oxford, the tour travels to Greenville and Clarksdale.

Mississippi Delta Cultural Tour, contact Jimmy Thomas at 662-915-3374 (http://southernstudies.olemiss.edu)

ᕲ Jackson

I think now, in looking back on these summer trips—this one and a number later, made in the car and on the train—that another element in them must have been influencing my mind. The trips were wholes unto themselves. They were stories. Not only in form, but in their taking on direction, movement, development, change. They changed something in my life: each trip made its particular revelation, though I could not have found words for it. . . . When I did begin to write, the short story was a shape that had already formed itself and stood waiting in the back of my mind.

—EUDORA WELTY, *One Writer's Beginnings*

ONE OF THE FINEST SHORT-STORY WRITERS EVER, Eudora Welty traveled far and wide throughout her life, but the family home on Pinehurst Street in Jackson, where she lived for nearly 80 years, was where her imagination took flight. It was her beloved respite from 1925 until her death in 2001.

Welty's love of literature began in the family home on North Congress Street, where she spent her childhood surrounded by books by Mark Twain and Charles Dickens. Reading and storytelling were a way of life for the Welty family, with her father sitting in the parlor and reading one story after another to his children. "To both my parents," she wrote, "I owe my early acquaintance with a beloved Mark Twain. There was a full set of Mark Twain and a short set of Ring Lardner in our bookcase, and those were the volumes that in time united us all, parents and children." In 1925 at age 16 Welty along with her brothers and parents moved from the North Congress address into the Pinehurst home that is located in Jackson's Belhaven neighborhood.

Welty bequeathed the Pinehurst house to the state of Mississippi in 1999. The Tudor Revival home is listed on the National Register of Historic Places and remains completely intact. When Welty gave the house to the state, she did not want it to be about her but rather about her life and her writings. The Eudora Welty Foundation manages the house and was founded to oversee the archival material and preservation of the house. It has been meticulously restored to reflect the period when she was at the pinnacle of her literary success. When her father passed away in 1931, finances became so tight that in the 1950s she and her mother had to take in boarders to make ends meet. Her bedroom is filled with the books she loved and admired, including the works of William Faulkner, Virginia Woolf, and Anton Chekov. There are also a collection of photographs of her many writer friends, including Katherine Anne Porter, Reynolds Price, and E. M. Forster.

Her desk can also be seen on a visit. Like Hemingway, Wolfe, and Fitzgerald, Welty composed everything in longhand before typing on her Royal typewriter. All the books, photographs, and furniture in the house belonged to her. If the house exhibits her soul as a writer, the gardens reveal her heart. "I like to work in the yard," she said in 1946. "I never get tired, and can think there, or maybe it's dreaming." The garden was as much a part of her life as her books and writing and became an essential part of her life after she lost her father. She and her mother spent hours in the garden to ease their sorrow. Camellias, azaleas, daylilies, and crepe myrtle accent its southern charm. It has been restored to reflect the period from 1925 to 1945 when she and her mother worked tirelessly to improve its appearance. In "The Perfect Garden" she noted that "The loved garden . . . flaunts its colors joyously when we are glad, its peace and fragrance are soothing to frayed nerves when we are weary from contact or perhaps conflict with the everyday world, and its recurrent beauty whispers a message of comfort and hope when our hearts are lonely or sorrowful."

Another Welty site is the local library that was named in her honor in 1991. She spent considerable time at the old Carnegie Library. Her mother advised the librarian, Mrs. Callaway, that her daughter could read any books she wanted. Inside the **Eudora Welty Library** is a handsome display in the Mississippi Writers Room that honors Mississippi poets, playwrights, and writers who made a difference. Photographs of William Faulkner, Margaret Walker Alexander, Richard Wright, Tennessee Williams, Walker Percy, and Shelby Foote, along with Eudora Welty, are on display in this room. Copies of their works are also found on the shelves, along with facts about their writing lives.

Eudora Welty House, 1119 Pinehurst Street, Jackson, MS 39202 (601-353-7762; www.eudorawelty.org)

Eudora Welty Library, 300 North State Street, Jackson, MS 39201 (601-968-5813)

🍸 LITERARY LODGING

THE FAIRVIEW INN

The Fairview Inn sits in the center of the Belhaven neighborhood not too far from Eudora Welty's home. Dating back to 1908, it was a fixture in Welty's world during her most prolific years. It offers 18 rooms and Sophia's Restaurant. The AAA Four-Diamond inn is Jackson's most historic, and listed on the National Register of Historic Places.

Fairview Inn, 734 Fairview Street, Jackson, MS 39202 (601-948-3429 or 1-888-948-1908; www.fairviewinn.com)

⚙ EXCURSIONS AND DIVERSIONS

EXPLORING JACKSON

Jackson is Mississippi's state capital and filled with sites to explore. The **Old Capitol Museum,** now a National Historic Landmark, has been restored to its original glory and features an array of exhibits. Admission is free, and tours can be scheduled for groups of 10 and more. The **Governor's Mansion** is the second oldest such mansion in the United States. During the Civil War it was occupied by Union troops. The mansion fell into decline until 1908, when its first renovation took place. Another outing could include the **Mississippi Museum of Art,** the areas' newest cultural venue, with an extensive collection of French paintings.

Jackson CVB, 111 East Capitol Street, Jackson, MS 39201 (601-960-1891 or 1-800-354-7695; www.visitjackson.com)

Old Capitol Museum, 100 South State Street, Jackson, MS 39201 (601-576-6920; http://mdah.state.ms.us/oldcap/index.php)

Governor's Mansion, 300 East Capitol Street, Jackson, MS 39201 (601-359-6421; http://mdah.state.ms.us/museum/govtour.html)

Mississippi Museum of Art, 380 South Lamar Street, Jackson, MS 39201 (601-960-1515; www.msmuseumart.org)

MARGARET WALKER ALEXANDER
AND RICHARD WRIGHT

Jackson also pays tribute to Margaret Walker Alexander, author of *Jubilee*, who is remembered at the **Margaret Walker Center** at Jackson State University, where African American history is preserved through archival records. Richard Wright, the author of *Native Son* and *Black Boy*, is another prominent African American writer with Jackson roots. Born near Natchez, Mississippi, the future author moved to Jackson as a child. The **Richard Wright Library** honors him.

Margaret Walker Center, Jackson State University, Ayer Hall, 1400 J. R. Lynch Street, Jackson, MS 39217 (601-979-3935; www.jsums.edu/margaretwalker)

Richard Wright Library, 515 West McDowell Road, Jackson, MS 39204 (601-372-1621; www.jhlibrary.com/branches/shl.htm)

❧ Natchez

> There was the vague sense of the infinite as I looked down upon the yellow, dreaming waters of the Mississippi River from the verdant bluffs of Natchez.
>
> —RICHARD WRIGHT, *Black Boy*

THE OLDEST CITY ON THE MISSISSIPPI RIVER also happens to be one of the South's loveliest with its enviable collection of antebellum architecture and plantation homes. Founded in 1716, Natchez's economy was derived from cotton and sugar. Steamboats once plied its waters, with riverboat gamblers arriving almost daily prior to the outbreak of the Civil War.

With the advent of the railroad and aftermath of the Civil War, Natchez fell into serious decline. Today, however, the town is a showplace for southern architecture and culture. There are 11 historic homes open for touring; perhaps the most famous is the octagonal **Longwood,** with its associations to the Civil War. Natchez is also where Jefferson Davis got married for the second time at the Briars B&B, which continues to host guests. The Natchez Trace, a winding parkway stretching from south to north for 444 miles, is one of the South's geographic centerpieces.

African American writer Richard Wright, the grandson of a slave, was born on the Rucker Plantation on September 4, 1908, just outside Natchez. A historic plaque in the center of town pays tribute to the writer, as does the Richard Wright Memorial Highway.

Wright, raised by his grandmother in Jackson, began writing as a teenager. His first story, "The Voodoo of Hell's Half-Acre," was published in the *Southern Register,* a Mississippi newspaper for African Americans. His writing career took him to Chicago and New York, where he developed a close friendship with Ralph Ellison. Wright's *Native Son* was published in 1940. John A. Williams, author of the Wright biography *The Most Native of Sons,* wrote that "the wounds of segregation in the Deep South and throughout the country always followed him."

Longwood, 140 Lower Woodville Road, Natchez, MS 39120 (www.stantonhall.com)

Natchez CVB, 640 S. Canal Street, Natchez, MS 39120 (1-800-647-6724, www.visitnatchez.org)

⑤ LITERARY LODGING

THE BRIARS BED & BREAKFAST
The Briars B&B is where Jefferson Davis, president of the Confederacy, married Varina Howell in 1845; it was her family home. A classic antebellum home and a National Historic Landmark, it overlooks a scenic bluff—the highest promontory point above the Mississippi. In the spring more than 1,000 azaleas and camellias accent its stunning landscape. The inn has suites named after Davis and Howell. There is also a restaurant on the premises specializing in southern cuisine.

The Briars B&B, 31 Irving Lane, Natchez, MS 39120 (601-653-0017 or 1-888-609-1127; www.thebriarsbb.com)

⤳ Oxford

It was a summer of wisteria. The twilight was full of it and of the smell of his father's cigar as they sat on the front gallery after supper until it would be time for Quentin to start, while in the deep shaggy lawn below the veranda the fireflies blew and drifted in soft random.
—WILLIAM FAULKNER, *Absalom, Absalom!*

FEW AMERICAN AUTHORS can stand alongside William Faulkner in terms of literary greatness.

Oxford, two hours south of Memphis, is Faulkner country. Everywhere you turn in this attractive college hamlet, you are met with the memories of "Mr. Bill"—the affectionate nickname given to him by the locals.

This corner of Mississippi with its rolling landscape and ghosts of Confederate soldiers became Faulkner's fictional Yoknapatawpha County, filled with colorful characters and memorable stories. From the town square where the southern writer spent countless hours observing people, to Lafayette Courthouse, to Rowan Oak, his literary sanctuary, and St. Peter's Cemetery where he is interred, the echoes of William Cuthbert Faulkner and his writings still sound.

Oxford became the canvas for Faulkner's novels. "Beginning with Sartoris," he wrote, "I discovered that my own little postage stamp of native soil was worth writing about and that I would never live long enough to exhaust it, and that by sublimating the actual into the apocryphal I would have complete liberty to use whatever talent I might have to its absolute top. It opened up a gold mine of other people, so I created a cosmos of my own."

Faulkner's literary prowess and success did not come easily. In 1924 he and his friend Phil Stone paid $400 to have his book of poetry *The Marble Faun* published. It was not until two years later that Faulkner completed his first novel, *Soldiers' Pay*, while living in New Orleans. It was also in New Orleans that Faulkner—acting on the advice of friend and author Sherwood Anderson—decided to head home and write about Oxford. Faulkner's works with their recurring southern themes make up an impressive body of work: *The Sound and the Fury, As I Lay Dying, Light in August, Requiem for a Nun,* and *A Fable,* among others. They might never have seen the light of day had he not traveled back to his "postage stamp of native soil."

ROWAN OAK
Courtesy of the Oxford Convention and Visitors Bureau

Rowan Oak, found off the Old Taylor Road about a mile from town, proves to be an irresistible beginning to your Faulkner excursion. He purchased the graceful white-columned house in 1930 and remained there until his death in 1962.

The house was in serious disrepair when he bought it, but he fell under its spell because it had a history and he thought that many southern ghosts had occupied its terrain. He undertook to renovate the old place and found the setting ideal for writing, pipe smoking, storytelling, and his life as a genteel southern gentleman. An avid horseman, he also spent many afternoons riding the land that nurtured his spirit and soul. He named it Rowan Oak after the rowan tree, which was believed to ward off evil spirits.

An archway of cedar trees frame the entranceway to this literary sanctuary, now managed by the University of Mississippi. You can almost imagine Faulkner attired in his familiar tweed jacket and cap surveying the land or taking long walks around its scenic perimeter.

In the living room a portrait of the writer hangs over the fireplace. Bookshelves display works by major 20th-century authors, including William Styron (*Lie Down in Darkness*) and Sinclair Lewis (*Elmer Gantry*). Also downstairs is the room where he outlined the plot of *A Fable* in pencil on the wall; his typewriter and smoking pipe rest nearby.

In one of the upstairs bedrooms his riding breeches are draped casually over a chair, while Estelle's room is much more ornate. Daughter Jill's room is also on the tour.

Faulkner treasured his time at Rowan Oak more than anyplace in the world and was reluctant to leave his corner of Mississippi—but in order to maintain his southern gentleman lifestyle he frequently traveled to California to work as a screenwriter. When home he frequently traveled to Memphis to buy his pipe tobacco or simply to enjoy observing guests at the Peabody Hotel (see the Tennessee chapter).

The Faulkners loved to entertain, and many friends spent the afternoon in their wooded retreat. Eudora Welty traveled from Jackson on two occasions to enjoy the family's company. On her first visit she wrote to friend Frank Lyell, "The house . . . has old wallpaper, soft old wood, a lovely patina—& I felt that *cool* you always said was in such houses in the country—Faulkner has three oil paintings stuck over his mantel, of himself & a lady and man, ancestors—all of whom look like Robert E. Lee—his mother painted them, I understand—and there is a bronze owl on his bookcase—He (F., not the owl) had on shorts & a blue shirt, had come in from seeing his race horse—which daughter Jill rides." Welty went on to describe Faulkner as "besides being the greatest writer to me, an attractive, darling person—quiet, listening to all kinds of stuff, amusing when he speaks."

On her return visit Welty expressed her respect and affection for the author once again. In a letter to Jean Stafford she wrote, "William Faulkner took us sailing on his sailboat on a big inland lake they've cut out of the woods there—waves and everything, big. We were late getting there—got lost and went to Blackjack, Miss.—and when we found the lake there was Faulkner, cruising around, and headed right for us, through the dead cypresses and stumps and all, pulled down his sail and took the oar, and hollered, 'You all better take your shoes off and get ready to wade,' which we did, sinking—got pulled on board and then we sailed around, all quiet and nice—what a wonderful person he is, the most profound face, something that nearly breaks your heart though, just in the clasp of his hand— a strange kind of life he leads in Oxford, two lives really. We never, either time I've been with him, talked about anything bookish of course—it's his life, not his opinions,—that seems to be with you all the time."

The Faulkner home also became the setting for many family events and festivities including the wedding receptions of his daughter, Jill, and niece Dean Faulkner Wells. On these important occasions Rowan Oak was bedecked in all its southern splendor, with champagne, mint juleps, a maze of flowers, and flowing organza dresses everywhere. Faulkner, a sentimentalist at heart, embraced southern customs and traditions, and a crucial one was that everyone was expected to dress for dinner. The bourbon flowed freely at the Faulkner residence, particularly on New Year's Eve when he gave his familiar toast to guests: "Here's to the younger generation, may you profit from the mistakes of your elders." Younger guests in attendance were allowed to have one glass of champagne to ring in the New Year. And "Pappy"—the name given to him by his family—loved to spin one ghost story after another. Mr. Bill had assumed the guise of a respectable Mississippi gentleman at Rowan Oak.

Rowan Oak was also the location for Faulkner's funeral. He passed away on July 6, 1962, from complications following a riding accident. His death shattered many in the literary world as well as the people of Oxford, who had come to know and respect him. He was laid to rest at **St. Peters Cemetery,** Jefferson at North 16th Street, where all

of his kinfolk were buried. Businesses closed and citizens with "watchful and brooding faces"—as William Styron described it in his *Life* magazine essay—turned toward the motorcade that passed through town and paid their last respects. Faulkner's description of a funeral in *Go Down Moses* in fact closely matched his own. "Into the square," he wrote of the funeral procession, "crossing it, circling the Confederate monument and the courthouse while the merchants and clerks and barbers and professional men . . . watched quietly from the doors of upstairs windows."

FAULKNER WAS LAID TO REST AT
ST. PETER'S CEMETERY

With Faulkner's death some felt that a little bit of the South that he had known, loved, and memorialized had changed and almost disappeared. His legacy, however, lives on in Oxford. His grave site at St. Peter's is inscribed "Belov'd, Go with God." Other Faulkner sites in Oxford include a bronze sculpture of him sitting on a bench outside **Oxford City Hall** and the **Lafayette County Courthouse,** 1 Courthouse Square, which he was instrumental in saving from destruction; it is now fully restored. The courthouse is mentioned in *Requiem for a Nun*; inscribed on a bronze plaque are words from the novel: "But above all, the courthouse: the center, the focus, the hub; sitting looming in the center of the county's circumference like a single cloud in its ring of horizon." The statue of the Confederate soldier with "empty eyes," mentioned in *The Sound and the Fury,* can also be viewed at this site.

The **University Post Office,** now Fraser Hall on Pierce Avenue, is where he worked as a postmaster beginning in 1921. Fired from the position for reading magazines and playing cards, Faulkner was relieved when he was let go: "I refuse to place myself at the beck and call of every S.O.B. with the price of a two-cent stamp." **Phil Stone's office** at 1013 Jackson Avenue is where Stone and Faulkner prepared the first manuscript of *A Marble Faun.* **College Hill Presbyterian Church** on County Road is where he and Estelle were married on June 20, 1929. Listed on the National Register of Historic Places, it is the oldest church in the county.

The **J. D. Williams Library,** 1 Library Loop, houses the William Faulkner Collection, including his Nobel Prize. The Compson House, now known as the **Thompson-Chandler House,** 923 South 13th Street, is believed to have been the model for the home of Benjy Compson in *The Sound and the Fury.* Faulkner's childhood home is located on Lincoln Avenue; it is now a private residence. It is not far from the Duvall house, near 9th Street, which Faulkner rented a portion of when he was first married. **Duvall's,** 103 Courthouse Square, was originally the First National Bank, where Faulkner's paternal grandfather worked as a bookkeeper.

St. Peter's Episcopal Church, 113 South 9th Street, is where Faulkner attended church and where his daughter Jill was married. The **University of Mississippi Museum** has an exhibit on Faulkner and also arranges guided tours of Rowan Oak.

> **Rowan Oak,** Old Taylor Road, Oxford, MS 38665 (662-234-3284; www.rowanoak.com)

> **University of Mississippi Museum,** University Avenue and 5th Street, Oxford, MS 38655 (662-915-7073; http://museum .olemiss.edu)

> **Oxford CVB,** 102 Ed Perry Blvd, Oxford, MS 38655 (662-232-2367, 1-800-758-9177, www.oxfordcvb.com)

🍸 LITERARY LODGING

OXFORD ACCOMMODATIONS

Faulkner's own favorite place to stay was the Peabody Hotel in Memphis, Tennessee; see chapter 9 for full details. If you want to stay close to Oxford on your visit, one ideal choice is **The Inn at Ole Miss,** which sits on the campus on its own 11 acres. You can easily walk to downtown and most of the Faulkner sites.

For a more unusual setting evoking the barns that were once predominant in Mississippi, Tennessee, and Kentucky, the **Willowdale Farm** is a good choice. The barn loft B&B is on 33 acres and is easily accessible from Oxford.

The Inn at Ole Miss, 120 Alumni Drive, University, MS 38677 (662-234-2331 or 1-888-486-7666; www.theinnatolemiss.com)

Willowdale Farm, 28 County Road 225, Oxford, MS 38655
(662-513-3662; www.thefarmatwillowdale.com)

⚙ EXCURSIONS AND DIVERSIONS

BOOKS AND BOOK EVENTS

On any trip to Oxford, **Square Books** is a must for bibliophiles.
Many noted authors do book signings at this historic independent
bookstore, which also carries an abundance of Faulkner's works and
those of other major southern writers.

Annually the University of Mississippi hosts the **Faulkner and
Yoknapatawpha Conference** in July—a five-day event that includes
lectures, seminars, and tours to Oxford and Faulkner sites.

Another annual event for Faulkner fans in Oxford is the **Oxford
Conference for the Book,** which encompasses three days of programs centered on Faulkner and southern writers. The three-day
event entering its 20th year in 2013, offers readings and seminars;
it's free and open to the public.

Square Books, 160 Courthouse Square, Oxford, MS 38655
(662-236-2262; www.squarebooks.com)

Faulkner and Yoknapatawpha Conference (www.outreach
.olemiss.edu/events/faulkner)

Oxford Conference for the Book, contact Becca Walton at
662-915-5993 (www.oxfordconferenceforthebook.com)

NEW ALBANY—BIRTHPLACE OF WILLIAM FAULKNER

Prior to his family moving to Oxford, William Faulkner was born
in New Albany, Mississippi, on September 25, 1897. The town is
approximately 75 miles from Memphis. A plaque can be found at
the **Union County Heritage Museum,** where the tranquil Faulkner
Literary Garden is located. This peaceful enclave is marked by a profusion of flowers and a walkway that includes words from his many
works. There is also an exhibit on the writer and many of his works,
including *The Reivers.*

Union County Heritage Museum, 114 Cleveland Street, New
Albany, MS 38652 (662-538-0014; www.ucheritagemuseum
.com)

NORTH CAROLINA

T HERE IS SOMETHING ABOUT the "Carolina Blue" sky that hovers above the Tar Heel State—the moniker comes from a time when tar, pitch, and turpentine were produced from its pine forests—that has attracted a range of writers.

Its history spans from the English settlements of Sir Walter Raleigh to the suspense and drama of the Civil War. Many of its men fought alongside with General Robert E. Lee's Virginia army at the Battle of Gettysburg, where two-thirds of the casualties were North Carolinians. Kitty Hawk on the Outer Banks is where the pioneers of flight, Wilbur and Orville Wright, launched the first successful airplane. Blackbeard and his pirates invaded the shores at Ocracoke.

Often referred to as a "valley of humility between two mountains of conceit," North Carolina retains its relaxed southern flavor at an abundant of lovely coastal communities from New Bern to Manteo. Wilmington is the second largest film industry center outside Los Angeles, adding to the state's cultural awareness. Cutting-edge medicine is practiced at both Duke University and the University of North Carolina at Chapel Hill, the oldest state university in the nation.

At the very heart of this southern state is the tobacco crop that created the Duke and Reynolds family fortunes in Durham and Winston-Salem. North Carolina's geographic diversity is the envy of the South, encompassing both the Atlantic Ocean and the mountains encircling Asheville. The Cape Hatteras National Seashore on the Outer Banks is the nation's first national seashore, with some 30,000 acres.

A collection of esteemed writers has traveled, studied, and lived in this state. Manteo is the site of Paul Green's long-running outdoor play *The Lost Colony.* Asheville and Chapel Hill reflect the indomitable spirit of Wolfe's *Look Homeward, Angel.* From O. Henry's to William Styron and Reynolds Price, F. Scott Fitzgerald and poet Carl Sandburg, a North Carolina literary tour could prove to be your favorite.

ᴄᴡ Asheville

> *Some day someone will write a book about a man who was too tall. . . .*
> *It is a strange adventure—the adventure of being very tall—and in*
> *its essence it comes to have a singular and instinctive humanity. In an*
> *extraordinary way, a tall man comes to know things about the world*
> *as other people do not, cannot, know them.*
>
> —Thomas Wolfe,
> "Gulliver: The Story of a Tall Man"

THOMAS WOLFE
Courtesy of the Thomas Wolfe Memorial State Historic Site

A SOFT BLUE MIST SHIMMERS in the morning light in Asheville, particularly in the fall when the mountains are ablaze with brilliant autumn colors.

Largely associated with George Vanderbilt's palatial Biltmore Estate, Asheville is perhaps most famous for being the boyhood hometown of Thomas Wolfe, who was born here in 1900. Wolfe poignantly captured his childhood memories in his first autobiographical novel, *Look Homeward, Angel.*

This gentle giant who clearly casts the longest literary shadow in Asheville is joined by Jazz Age novelist F. Scott Fitzgerald, poet Carl

Sandburg, and Charles Frazier, best known for his Civil War tale, *Cold Mountain*. Gilded Age authors Edith Wharton and Henry James also have an Asheville connection—both were guests at the Vanderbilt Estate. And William Sydney Porter (O. Henry) is, along with Thomas Wolfe, interred at Riverside Cemetery.

In this mountain hamlet on the fringes of the Great Smoky Mountains, Wolfe's memory and larger-than-life legacy are found everywhere, from the bronze angel memorial at the entrance to the to the Pack Center for the Arts to the Old Kentucky Home downtown.

Today the city embraces Wolfe with great zeal. But he was not always seen as the hometown hero. Following the publication of *Look Homeward, Angel* in 1929, family and friends scorned the novel for portraying Asheville and its citizens in an unflattering light. Wolfe's honest picture of the provincial North Carolina town proved a burden to Asheville for many

WOLFE'S OLD KENTUCKY HOME
Courtesy of the Thomas Wolfe Memorial State Historic Site

years and prevented Wolfe from returning until his final visit in 1937.

The Old Kentucky Home on Market Street—Wolfe's family home—is dwarfed by the towering skyscrapers that surround it, but a visit offers a clear perspective into Wolfe's childhood in Asheville. The pages of *Look Homeward, Angel* spring to life here. Built in 1883, the Queen Anne Victorian home re-captures Asheville's past; gables, faded stained-glass windows, and rocking chairs on the porch accent its melancholy ambience.

A contemporary visitors center that opened in 1998 makes an ideal introduction into Wolfe's life and writings. A brief but compelling video provides an overview of his life. Several rooms in the center are filled with an array of artifacts—vintage family photographs, quotes from other authors who knew him, his Remington typewriter—from his Asheville years, travels, and writing life. His complex relationships with both his editor, Max Perkins, and love interest, Aline Bernstein, are studied on the tour. Memorabilia from his New York apartment at the Chelsea Hotel is also on display.

Following your self-guided tour through the visitors center, a docent will walk you through the Victorian home where Wolfe lived from 1906 until 1916. Named "Dixieland" in the novel, Wolfe wrote that the house "was situated five minutes from the public square, on a pleasant sloping middle-class street of small homes and boarding-houses. Dixieland was a big cheaply constructed frame house of eighteen to twenty drafty high-ceilinged rooms: it had a rambling, unplanned, gabular appearance, and was painted a dirty yellow. It had a pleasant green front yard not deep but wide, bordered by a row of young maples."

Wolfe's mother, Julia Wolfe, used the home as a boardinghouse for strangers, adding to her income but preventing her children from enjoying a warm and happy home life. The youngest of eight children, Wolfe described his life in the house as an extremely lonely experience. His parents lived apart, shuttled young Tom between the boardinghouse and the home of his father, W. O. Wolfe, several blocks away. Growing up, he had to contend with changing bedrooms almost on a daily basis to accommodate the paying customers. Family life was confusing for the youth, whose favorite room was the upstairs sleeping porch. He also worked as a paperboy, and his mother gave him business cards to solicit customers for the boarding-house. As a boy Wolfe often dreamed of travel when he heard trains traveling through Asheville in the dark of night.

He inherited a love of literature from his father and was an outstanding student, entering the University of North Carolina in Chapel Hill at age sixteen. In effect, at a very young age Thomas Wolfe escaped into the world of books to satisfy his creative longings. His favorite brother Ben served as his protector and surrogate father during his childhood. Ben's room upstairs, with its gloomy Victorian windows and dark and foreboding atmosphere, reveals a traumatic chapter in Wolfe's life. This is where Ben died in 1918 during the influenza epidemic. The wrought-iron bed remains today in the room where Wolfe saw his brother for the last time. In *Look Home-ward, Angel,* Wolfe vividly recalls his memories of the tragic experience and poignantly wrote, "Ben hurled into the darkness his savage curse at life. The light in the sick room burned grayly, bringing to him its grim vision of struggle and naked terror."

It was a turning point for Wolfe: "So, to Ben dead was given more care, more time,

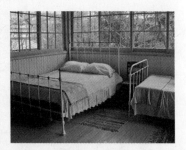

INSIDE WOLFE'S OLD KENTUCKY HOME
Courtesy of the Thomas Wolfe Memorial State Historic Site

more money than had ever been given to Ben living. . . . And as the wind howled in the bleak street and Eliza wove a thousand fables of that lost and bitter spirit, the bright and stricken thing in the boy twisted about in horror, looking for escape from the house of death. No More! No More! (It said). You are alone. You are lost. Go find yourself, lost boy, beyond the hills."

BRONZE REPLICA OF THOMAS WOLFE'S SHOES IN FRONT OF THE THOMAS WOLFE MEMORIAL
Courtesy of the Thomas Wolfe Memorial State Historic Site

In his later years Ben's death still haunted him, "I think the Asheville I knew," he wrote in a letter to his sister Mabel, "died for me when Ben died. I have never forgotten him and I never shall. I think his death affected me more than any other event in my life. . . . Ben—he was one of those fine people who want the best and highest out of life, and who got nothing—who die unknown and unsuccessful."

The downstairs rooms in the house were mainly used for dining and entertaining boarders. Today you can inspect Julia Wolfe's china and silverware. Artifacts including an upright piano in the parlor all belonged to the Wolfe family.

On Wolfe's final visit to Asheville in the summer of 1937 he lived in a small cabin just outside Asheville in Oteen, where he realized that he could not go home again; he had outgrown the small town's provinciality. While on an extended road trip out west to discover national parks, Wolfe became seriously ill while in Seattle and was diagnosed with tuberculosis of the brain. With his family and his loyal editor Max Perkins by his side, Wolfe passed away on a fall morning in September 1938 at Baltimore's Johns Hopkins University Hospital. He was carried back to the city of his birth by train for his funeral at the **First Presbyterian Church,** with playwright and fellow North Carolina author Paul Green serving as an honorary pallbearer. Buried at **Riverside Cemetery** in the city's Montford Historic District, the writer who immortalized Asheville in many of his writings had come home again. Of his passing Fitzgerald commented in a letter to Maxwell Perkins, "There is a great hush after him"; "that great pulsing, vital frame quiet at last."

The epitaph on his gravestone reads, "The last voyage, the longest, the best," from *Look Homeward, Angel,* and "Death bent to touch his chosen son with mercy, love and pity, and put the seal of honor on him when he died," from *The Web and the Rock.*

Other Wolfe-related sites in Asheville include the **Jackson Building** where W. O. Wolfe had his stonecutting business, found at 22 Pack Square in downtown Asheville. This building was the first skyscraper in North Carolina. Built in 1924, the Neo-Gothic building is near the bronze angel dedicated by the Daughters of the Confederacy to honor Thomas Wolfe at the **Pack Center for the Arts.**

Thomas Wolfe Memorial, 52 North Market Street, Asheville (828-253-8304; www.wolfememorial.com)

Fitzgerald in Asheville

Contemporaries, colleagues, and literary friends sharing the same editor, Max Perkins, for several years, Thomas Wolfe and F. Scott Fitzgerald frequently corresponded. In the summers of 1935 and 1936 the *Great Gatsby* author arrived in Asheville to reclaim his shattered life. His reasons were threefold: His wife, Zelda, was being treated at Highlands Hospital; doctors had diagnosed a small spot on Fitzgerald's lung and feared tuberculosis; and Fitzgerald felt the area, would prove ideal for reigniting his flickering talent. The writer who had captivated a generation with *This Side of Paradise* and *The Beautiful and the Damned* had been challenged on every emotional level.

Hidden down a winding mountain roadway but not too distant from downtown and the Old Kentucky Home is the **Grove Park Inn** (see the "Literary Lodging" sidebar). The novelist lived in rooms 441–443.

Fitzgerald chose those rooms—an adjoining parlor and bedroom—for a variety of reasons. For one, there was a staircase nearby where he could make easy exits to avoid the glaring eyes of the public. In addition, the suite overlooked the driveway; he could peer out the window and witness all of the hotel's activity. Today a small plaque outside the room has Fitzgerald's name engraved on it,

THE GROVE PARK INN

with many fans of the novelist frequently requesting the room. Photographs of the author adorn its walls and tours are given during the Fitzgerald Weekend in September.

The imposing lobby with its large stone boulders seems grand enough to have attracted the Jay Gatsby's of Fitzgerald's generation—and indeed it did: Harvey Firestone Sr., auto magnate Henry Ford, and John D. Rockefeller, who visited the hotel while overseeing the development of the Great Smoky Mountains National Park, all visited the inn.

Stories of Fitzgerald's time in Asheville still swirl today. It is rumored that while staying in the hotel he enjoyed a series of romantic dalliances, one quite serious. In a letter to friend James Boyd, he wrote, "I have just emerged not totally unscathed, I'm afraid, from a short violent love affair . . . ," he wrote. "I had done much better to let it alone because this was scarcely a time in my life for one more emotion. Still it's done now and tied up in cellophane and—maybe someday I'll get a chapter out of it. God, what a hell of a profession to be a writer."

Fitzgerald loved to sit out on the back porch and gaze out at the misty blue mountains that surrounded the inn. On several occasions he took day trips to nearby Lake Lure and Chimney Rock Park to pass the time. On one outing into town he purchased a copy of *Look Homeward, Angel* and donated it to the public library.

Fitzgerald's desire to pen another novel in Asheville proved fruitless; his creative output consisted mainly of short magazine pieces and an occasional short story. On one evening he ventured out to Hendersonville and packed a briefcase to attempt writing. This endeavor led to *Crack-Up*, essays originally published in *Esquire* magazine. Of this experience he wrote, "One harassed and despairing night I packed a briefcase and went a thousand miles to think it over. I took a dollar room in a drab little town and sunk all the money I had with me in a stock of potted meat, crackers, and apples. . . . I began to realize that for two years of my life I had been drawing resources that I did not possess, that I had been mortgaging myself to the hilt."

Realizing that Zelda was beyond recovery, Fitzgerald left Asheville in the summer of 1936, signaling the end of his marriage. He would return briefly to visit her, but in time even that ended. From Asheville he traveled back to New York and eventually to California where he worked on his final, unfinished novel, *The Last Tycoon*.

Edith Wharton and Henry James at the Biltmore Estate

The journey here was frightfully fatiguing, but this divine landscape,
"under a roof of blue Ionian weather," makes up for all of the hardship.
—EDITH WHARTON

EDITH WHARTON AND HENRY JAMES were close friends and enjoyed visiting George Vanderbilt's opulent estate in Asheville. Biltmore is by far the grandest literary stop in Asheville, but well worth a visit for the chance to witness the glory of the Gilded Age.

Millionaires can dare to dream without limits, and George Vanderbilt did just that when he built Biltmore—North Carolina's most visited attraction, still owned and managed by his ancestors. Recruiting the great talents of Richard Morris Hunt and Frederick Law Olmsted, Biltmore was constructed between 1889 and 1895. The 250-room mansion is the largest private home in the United States.

Vanderbilt was an avid book collector and admirer of literary talent; his library held thousands of volumes, including titles by both Edith Wharton and Henry James—both of whom he invited to his mountain hideaway. Wharton arrived for Christmas 1905. After spending several days at the wooded estate, she inscribed a copy of her novel *The House of Mirth* to Vanderbilt. In a letter following her visit, she wrote to friend Sara Norton, "Yesterday we had a big Christmas fete for the 350 people on the estate—a tree 30-feet high, a Punch and Judy conjuror, presents and refreshments."

Henry James's view was less sentimental. In a letter to Wharton he wrote, "I can't tell you meanwhile how mighty I think it of you to be spending the Christmastide at Biltmore. . . . May those marble halls not expand, but *contract*, to receive you, and may you have, as you of course will, one of the *apartements* of state, and not a bachelor bedroom, as I did, in the wing looking over an ice-bound stable-yard, and that even the blaze of felled tree didn't warm. But there must be always this about Biltmore, that it thoroughly fills the mind, while one is there—little as the mind can do to fill *it*."

GEORGE VANDERBILT'S BILTMORE ESTATE
Photo by Ken Thomas. Wikimedia Commons, p.d.

The house that Vanderbilt built offers a range of tours, including a Behind-the-Scenes Tour that relives the glory of the Gilded Age and some of the characters who visited the estate, including Edith Wharton and Henry James. The holiday season is the ideal time to enjoy what Wharton might have experienced on her visit.

The Biltmore Estate is a day's outing in itself, with tours through the main house, gardens, winery, and history gallery on offer. All things of or about the Vanderbilts can be seen and studied in this French chateau mansion filled with priceless paintings and furnishings. A range of restaurants and an ice cream parlor from the Biltmore Creamery make this an ideal choice following your Thomas Wolfe excursion. The inn on the premises recalls the Gilded Age.

Biltmore Estate, 1 Lodge Street, Asheville, NC 28803 (1-800-411-3812; www.biltmore.com)

⊛ EXCURSIONS AND DIVERSIONS

EXPLORING ASHEVILLE

Asheville is rich in literary connections—but there is far more to explore in and around this city as well. One additional stop should bethe **Folk Art Center** on the Blue Ridge Parkway. Home to the Southern Highland Craft Guild, the center features some of the finest in both traditional and contemporary crafts of the Southern Appalachians. Also within close proximity are the **Great Smoky Mountains National Park** and the **Pisgah National Forest.** North Carolina's section of the Great Smokies includes Clingman's Dome, the highest point in the park. The scenery along this stretch of the park is breathtaking in the autumn.

Folk Art Center, Milepost 382 Blue Ridge Parkway, Asheville, NC (828-298-7928; www.southernhighlandguild.org)

Great Smoky Mountains National Park (www.nps.gov/grsm)

Pisgah National Forest (www.fs.usda.gov/recarea/nfsnc /recarea/?recid=48114)

Asheville CVB, 36 Montford Avenue, Asheville, NC 28801 (828-258-6101, www.exploreasheville.com)

§ LITERARY LODGING

THE GROVE PARK INN

The sprawling Grove Park Inn resort is Asheville's most historic and can claim F. Scott Fitzgerald as its most lionized literary guest. Rooms 441–443, where he stayed on his sojourn here, can be reserved for an overnight stay—but be forewarned that they are usually booked on the Fitzgerald Weekend in September.

The story of the inn's beginnings is as big and bold as the boulders that were used in its construction. Edwin Wiley Grove, a Tennessean who made his money in a St. Louis pharmaceutical firm, hired a team of artisans and hundreds of Italian stonemasons to realize his seemingly impossible dream. The lobby's massive boulders were taken from Asheville's Sunset Mountain and transported to the site by wagon train. On July 12, 1912, the official groundbreaking was held, and just 11 months later the Grove Park Inn opened its doors to the public. Williams Jennings Bryan delivered the keynote address, saying, "Today we stand in this wonderful hotel, not built for a few, but the multitudes that will come and go. I congratulate these men. They have built for the ages."

In addition to Fitzgerald, other guests of note at the posh retreat have included Presidents Franklin and Teddy Roosevelt, golfer Bobby Jones, and Margaret Mitchell, who honeymooned at the inn in 1922 with her first husband Red Upshaw. The Mobil Four-Star, AAA Four-Diamond property offers a spa, wine tasting weekends, gold packages, and an indoor/outdoor pool.

Grove Park Inn, 290 Macon Avenue, Asheville, NC 28804 (828-252-2711; www.groveparkinn.com)

ᥱ Flat Rock

I make it clear why I write as I do and why other people write as they do. After hundreds of experiments I decided to go my own way in style and see what would happen.

—CARL SANDBURG

JUST 27 MILES FROM ASHEVILLE is Flat Rock, where you'll find Connemara—Carl Sandburg's 264-acre estate. The house itself is a white frame cottage built in 1838 by Christopher Memminger, secretary of the treasury for the Confederacy. Subtle traces of its Old South lineage are visible in its graceful columned pillars and inviting porch. It all seems far removed from the poet who hailed from the Midwest and was a strong advocate of everyman.

CARL SANDBURG
Courtesy Library of Congress from New York World-Telegram & Sun Collection, Al Ravenna, photographer.

The story of how he became the "poet of the people" is quintessentially American. Sandburg, who won the Pulitzer Prize in 1940 for his six-volume biography of Abraham Lincoln, came to North Carolina not only to escape the bitter Chicago winters but also to raise goats with his wife, Lillian Paula Steichen. The peaceful setting offered a respite from Chicago's bright lights. At Connemara he would write, strum his guitar, and enjoy his family life.

A multimedia exhibit detailing his life begins your tour of the house. Sandburg, who began his journalism career at the *Chicago Daily News*, did most of his writing in the upstairs study where his familiar green eye shade, editing pencils, and notes are on view. Sandburg's Remington typewriter rests on a simple wooden grate. The downstairs rooms are filled with family photographs and mementos, including the guitar that rests beside his favorite chair. In the evenings Sandburg would serenade his daughters to unwind after a day of writing. Walls in the living room are lined with his extensive book collection, which includes some 11,000 volumes. Outside, 5 miles of hiking trails and meandering lanes wind around the bucolic property.

The house was donated to the National Park Service in 1965 following the poet's death—not only to protect and preserve the pastoral landscape but also to allow visitors to see his remarkable commitment to writing and poetry. Allow at least two hours to fully enjoy the estate, gardens, goat farm, and hiking trails.

Carl Sandburg Home National Historic Site, 81 Carl Sandburg Lane, Flat Rock, NC 28731 (828-693-4178; www.nps.gov/carl)

⚙ **EXCURSIONS AND DIVERSIONS**

THE STATE THEATRE OF NORTH CAROLINA

Flat Rock's State Theatre of North Carolina is a cultural venue—one of the state's oldest—featuring theater and musical concerts throughout the year, with the summer season the busiest. It's located just a few miles from Connemara and comprises the original barn playhouse in Flat Rock along with a downtown venue. Plays range from Neil Simon comedies to musical productions.

State Theatre of North Carolina, 2661 Greenville Highway, Flat Rock, NC 28731 (1-866-732-8008; www.flatrockplay house.org)

ᐤ Chapel Hill

> *The university was a charming, an unforgettable place. It was situated in the little village of Pulpit Hill, in the central midland of the big State. Students came and departed by motor from the dreary tobacco town of Exeter, twelve miles away: the countryside was raw, powerful and ugly, a rolling land of field, wood, and hollow; but the university itself was buried in a pastoral wilderness on a long tabling butte, which rose steeply above the country.*
>
> —THOMAS WOLFE, *Look Homeward, Angel*

IN THE AUTUMN OF 1916, as Thomas Wolfe stepped off the train in Durham to begin his college studies in Chapel Hill, he was filled with all of the hope, enthusiasm, and innocence of his generation. While his classmates were leaving for the war in Europe, Wolfe intently watched from the distant sidelines. When he arrived in Chapel Hill the student body consisted of 1,137 young people. Wolfe had originally wanted to go to Princeton, but his father convinced him that studying at UNC

Chapel Hill—the nation's oldest state university—would prepare him to study law.

In his 1920 yearbook, *The Yackety Yack*, Wolfe was described as follows: "Buck is a great big fellow. He can do more between 8:25 am and 8:30 am than the rest of us can do all day, it is no wonder he is classed as a genius." Unlike his contemporaries Ernest Hemingway and Scott Fitzgerald, who never finished college, Wolfe graduated in his 1920 class with honors and distinction. From the beginning of his undergraduate career he was a stellar student earning high marks in languages and English.

THOMAS WOLFE MEMORIAL AT UNIVERSITY OF NORTH CAROLINA, CHAPEL HILL

Wolfe, who named Chapel Hill "Pulpit Hill" in *Look Homeward, Angel*, expressed his fascination with college life in a letter to his mother, Julia, "I find myself," he wrote, "an evergrowing source of interest. Sounds egotistical, doesn't it? College life does more things for one than I would have ever dreamed."

Identified on campus by his commanding six-foot-seven stature, quick wit, casual and rumpled appearance, and late entrances to classes, Wolfe breezed through his undergraduate studies. His close friendships with Edwin Greenlaw, his English professor and teacher, and with Horace Williams, his philosophy teacher, only honed his intellect. Editing of the *Daily Tar Heel* and working on staff at *The Yackety Yack* polished his prose. He worked tirelessly on the student newspaper, crafting it into one of the best in the nation. It was not unusual for the ambitious Wolfe to catch an early bus to Durham, where the paper was published, and work well into the night until he put the paper to bed.

He was also very involved with Playmakers Theater and spent considerable time writing and acting in school productions, including his own play, *The Return of Buck Gavin*. Weekend jaunts to Richmond and Raleigh rounded out his active social life.

If he had entered Carolina as a shy and retiring freshman, by his senior year Wolfe had blossomed into one of the most charismatic personalities on campus, earning him the respect of his classmates.

THE OLD WELL, UNC CAMPUS

On graduation day his parents traveled from Asheville. He wrote in *Look Homeward, Angel,* "It was early June—hot, green, fiercely and voluptuously Southern. The campus was a green oven; the old grads went about in greasy pairs; the cool pretty girls, who never sweated, came in to see their young men graduate, and to dance. . . ."

Reluctant to leave Chapel Hill, Wolfe would head to Harvard and New York University after graduation carving out his career as a novelist and writer. In his later years he fondly recalled his days at Chapel Hill in a letter to friend and classmate Benjamin Cone: "So far from forgetting the blessed place, I think my picture of it grows clearer every year: it was as close to magic as I've ever been. . . ."

The Wolfe sites around campus are abundant. The **Wilson Library** has devoted a small room to him lined with a bronze bust, first editions, family photographs, and various memorabilia. The library itself also holds various Wolfe artifacts donated by the family. Around campus and outside Murphey Hall, a handsome red-brick monument to Wolfe includes a sculpture of an angel. Benches surround this peaceful place where students often sit and read between classes. The **Old Well** was another haunt for Wolfe, along with the **YMCA Building** on the oldest part of the campus and the original **Playmakers Theater.** Not far from here off Franklin Street is the **Horace Williams House.** Not only is this one

WILSON LIBRARY, UNC

of Chapel Hill's oldest and most historic houses, but it is where Wolfe would often drop in unexpectedly to visit his favorite professor.

University of North Carolina–Chapel Hill (919-962-2211; http://unc.edu)

Horace Williams House, 610 East Rosemary Street, Chapel Hill, NC 27514 (919-942-7818; http://preservationchapelhill.org)

CHAPEL HILL'S LITERARY ALUMS

In addition to Wolfe, the University of North Carolina has produced some of the South's most esteemed writers, journalists, and playwrights. Chapel Hill's library houses one of the most important southern culture collections in the nation, with significant artifacts and photographs pertaining to Shelby Foote, Walker Percy, and Robert Ruark—all graduates of the university, as was Richard Adler, author of *Damn Yankees* and *The Pajama Game*. A bust of playwright Paul Green is found outside the Paul Green Theater at Playmakers Theater inside the School of Dramatic Art. Charles Kuralt, who donated his newsroom office to the School of Journalism, is interred along with Green in the Chapel Hill Cemetery just outside Playmakers Theater.

UNC CAMPUS YMCA

✿ EXCURSIONS AND DIVERSIONS

MORE TO SEE IN CHAPEL HILL

On most days a "Carolina Blue" sky does indeed hover above the University of North Carolina campus, seeming to justify the familiar saying in this neck of the woods, "If God is not a Tarheel, then why is the sky Carolina Blue?" The school is set in Chapel Hill, a leafy college town that's one of the nation's prettiest.

Franklin Street is a winding boulevard framed by trees, intact antebellum homes, restaurants, and the **Morehead Planetarium,** all great places to explore. The **Ackland Art Museum** has rotating exhibits and a priceless collection of Rubens, Delacroix, and Degas paintings. The **Coker Arboretum** just behind the planetarium is an ideal place to view a lovely southern garden.

Morehead Planetarium (919-962-1236; www.morehead planetarium.org)

Ackland Art Museum (919-966-5636; www.ackland.org)

Coker Arboretum (919-962-0522; http://ncbg.unc.edu /coker-arboretum)

⚜ LITERARY LODGING

THE CAROLINA INN

Near the oldest part of UNC—which dates back to 1795—is the AAA Four-Diamond Carolina Inn. Owned and managed by the university and listed on the National Register of Historic Places, this is a prime spot to view tweedily attired professors, necktie-sporting alums, and students working as bartenders. Referred to as the "University's living room," and "the plushest dorm this side of Franklin Street," the inn opened in 1924 by University of North Carolina graduate John Sprunt Hill, who modeled it after Princeton's Nassau Inn. The inn has played host to a long list of luminaries including Eudora Welty, Walker Percy, Eleanor Roosevelt, and Andy Griffith, who got his singing start here.

The Carolina Inn, 211 Pittsboro Street, Chapel Hill, NC 27516 (1-866-974-3101, www.carolinainn.com)

ᐿ Durham

> *He worshipped literature. He saw it as a sustaining force in life. . . . We revered him because he made us see things we hadn't seen before. He was an illuminator.*
>
> —WILLIAM STYRON, SPEAKING ABOUT
> DUKE PROFESSOR WILLIAM BLACKBURN

THE GOTHIC ARCHITECTURE OF DUKE CHAPEL, with its soaring spires, recalls the university towns of England. Originally Trinity College, Duke was renamed for its benefactor, the industrialist James B. Duke, whose endowment facilitated the university's growth and expansion; today it ranks as one of the finest learning institutions in the world.

Many authors studied at Duke under the tutelage of Professor William Blackburn. His students included Reynolds Price (*Kate Vaiden*), Fred Chappell (*The Inkling*), Anne Tyler (*The Accidental Tourist*), and William Styron, perhaps the best-known writer of the group, author of the novels *Sophie's Choice* and *The Confessions of Nat Turner*, and the story collection *A Tidewater Morning.*

Styron came to Duke by happenstance. While at Davidson College in 1942, he wrote for both the school newspaper and the literary magazine. Shortly before his eighteenth birthday the Virginia-born writer enlisted in the US Marine Corps; in 1943 he transferred to Duke as part of an officer-training program. He served as a lieutenant in the marines, and after World War II he returned to Duke, studying under Blackburn, whom he credits with fueling his desire to write professionally. Following graduation in 1945 with a Bachelor of Arts in literature, he landed a job in New York at McGraw-Hill.

WILLIAM STYRON
Photo by William Waterway, 1989. Wikimedia Commons, p.d.

In his later years and several bestsellers later, Styron reflected on his writing process: "One of the most important aspects of writing is to establish characters that are real. If you can do that—that's more than half the battle." He added, "You can change over time, still it has always been kind of a calling. . . . a profession that I had to be involved with. . . . otherwise life would not have been worth living."

Styron bequeathed most of his most important manuscripts, papers, letters, and photographs to **Duke University's David M. Rubenstein Rare Book & Manuscript Library,** including the handwritten manuscript for *Sophie's Choice.*

Reynolds Price, a 1951 Duke graduate, went on to teach at the university for 50 years as a professor in the English Department. In 2008 a professorship in creative writing honoring Price was established. Price wrote in the *New York Times,* "The search for influences in a novelist's work is doomed to trivial results. A serious novelist's work is his effort to make from the chaos of all life, his life, strong though all-but-futile weapons, as beautiful, entire, true but finally helpless as the shield of Achilles itself." Price's students included Anne Tyler and Josephine Humphries.

After Price's death in January 2011, more than 300 people attended a memorial service at Duke Chapel to celebrate his life and literary achievements. A close friend of Eudora Welty's, Price left most of his letters, writings, and manuscripts to Rubenstein Library.

David M. Rubenstein Rare Book & Manuscript Library, Duke University, Durham, NC 27708 (919-660-5822; http://library.duke.edu/rubenstein)

ᐰ Greensboro

The true adventurer goes forth aimless and uncalculating to meet and greet unknown fate.

—O. HENRY

EDWARD R. MURROW
MEMORIAL

NORTH CAROLINA'S THIRD LARGEST CITY can lay claim to two renowned writers. William Sydney Porter (O. Henry) was born here, as was journalist Edward R. Murrow. Both writers are remembered at several sites in and around town.

At the height of the Civil War, William Sydney Porter was born in Guilford County. Three years later, in 1865, his family moved into Greensboro, the major city in Guilford, and lived on West Market Street.

Losing his mother at an early age left Will Porter in the care of his grandmother and his aunt Lina, who homeschooled the youth. His early years were marked with mischief, mayhem, and boyhood adventures. His love of the outdoors far outweighed his interest in schoolwork, but his love of reading grew as a result of Aunt Lina's tutelage.

At age 15 young Porter got his first job at his uncle's pharmacy at 121 South Elm. The day-to-day routine proved tedious to him, however, and he soon began dreaming about discovering new horizons. He got his first taste of adventure when a family friend, James Hale, invited the youth to accompany him on a trip to Texas. He leapt at the chance and soon fell in love with the vast Texas landscape. A writer was born. He started submitting stories to magazines, earning a little money, and in 1886 married Athol Estes. The newlyweds moved to Austin and became parents to Margaret Wolfe Porter. But Porter's life would take a turn for the worse when he secured a job as a bank teller at the First National Bank of Austin. During this period he was arrested for embezzlement; he was convicted and sentenced to five years at the Ohio Penitentiary.

The life-changing event propelled him to write stories from prison assuming the pen name O. Henry. Following prison he headed to New York and completed some of his most acclaimed work, including "Heart of the West," "Cabbages and Kings," "The Ransom of Red Chief," and

"The Gift of the Magi,"which catapulted him into literary prominence. His surprise endings became his trademark.

O. Henry is interred at Asheville's **Riverside Cemetery.** In 1918 the Society of Arts and Letters created the O. Henry Memorial Award, given annually to the best American short-story writer.

Traveling the **O. Henry Trail** in Greensboro is best accomplished by beginning at the **Greensboro Historical Museum** on Summit and Lindsay Streets. A detailed exhibit devoted to his life in Greensboro and literary career is found on the second floor. Vintage photographs, first editions, and personal letters

O. HENRY MEMORIAL

are on view in the attractive alcove setting. Across the hall is an exact replica of Miss Lina Porter's School, where you can view his schoolboy desk. Also in this area is a replica of the downtown pharmacy he worked in. Outside the museum is a life-sized stone statue of O. Henry as a youth; the author's

O. HENRY MEMORIAL

parents and grandparents are interred in the graveyard behind the museum.

A few short blocks from here at **440 West Market Street** is a North Carolina Historical Marker denoting the site where his family home was located. The most moving and elaborate memorial to the writer is found at **301 North Elm Street.** A life-sized bronze three-part sculpture created by artist Maria J. Kirby in 1985: an open book with a young lad looking on, a dog, and a life-sized sculpture of O. Henry writing in his notebook.

FROM GREENSBORO TO LONDON

Greensboro lays claim to being the hometown of journalist Edward R. Murrow, who won fame for his radio broadcasts from London during World War II and as a pioneer of television news. Murrow was born in Polecat Creek just outside Greensboro in 1908. He is remembered in a bust found outside the Greensboro Historical Museum.

⚘ LITERARY LODGING

O. HENRY HOTEL

Named after William Sydney Porter, this lovely boutique hotel in the Arts and Crafts style was constructed specifically to honor the city's most famous writer. An oil painting of O. Henry hangs in the lobby, which resembles a turn-of-the-century living room. The hotel's plushest suites celebrate the writer's legacy. The Porter and Magi Suites are the most opulent. Inside each you'll find a fireplace, living room, and two bedrooms furnished with honey pine furniture as well as a terrazzo shower. All of the rooms in the hotel have a book of O. Henry's stories on the nightstand. Residents and owners Dennis and Nancy Quaintance infuse the hotel with a genuine sense of graciousness and Southern hospitality from the moment you step inside the doors. The original O. Henry Hotel was demolished in the 1970s; although this new version is only 10 years old, it has successfully recaptured O. Henry's era in its design.

O. Henry Hotel, 624 Green Valley Road, Greensboro, NC 27408 (336-854-2000; www.ohenryhotel.com)

⚘ EXCURSIONS AND DIVERSIONS

GREENSBORO HIGHLIGHTS

Greensboro is North Carolina's third largest city and is also one of the most richly endowed with cultural and outdoor options. Get a taste of the Revolutionary War at the **Guilford Courthouse National Military Park** roughly 20 minutes from downtown Greensboro. The vast wooded battlefield is dotted with historic figures pertaining to the battle, including Major General Nathaniel Greene, the city's namesake; a walking tour through the site allows you to view them up close. In the springtime abundant flowers blanket the park. A film and book shop round out a visit.

Another exceptional forest setting is found at the **Bog Garden,** a nature preserve, botanical garden and city park where barred owls, ospreys, and northern shovelers are in residence. An elevated wooden boardwalk winds its way along a scenic pathway at this popular weekend spot.

Guilford Courthouse National Military Park, 2332 New Garden Road, Greensboro, NC 27410-2355 (336-288-1776; www.nps.gov/guco)

Bog Garden, 1101 Hobbs Road, Greensboro, NC 27410 (www.greensborobeautiful.org/gardens/bog_garden.php)

∾ Manteo

THE TOWN OF MANTEO is located on Roanoke Island in the Outer Banks. This historic island with its windswept beaches, vintage lighthouses, and legends of the pirate Blackbeard played a major part in the Civil War; Union forces captured it in 1862. It is also where one of the first English settlements landed in the New World, inspiring dramatist Paul Green to pen *The Lost Colony.*

The play is now produced in the summer at the Waterside Theatre, which overlooks Croatan Sound. A bust of Green is found at the amphitheater entrance. The tradition of annual performances began in 1921, the exception being during World War II when German U-boats plied the Atlantic. In 1936 President Franklin Roosevelt attended the drama when he was visiting the Outer Banks. The theater is part of Fort Raleigh National Historic Site, which consists of the Elizabethan Gardens, Freedman's Colony, and a visitor center that tells the story of the Lost Colony and the Roanoke Voyages.

Green, a native of Hartnett County and drama professor at the University of North Carolina–Chapel Hill, was the recipient of the Pulitzer Prize in 1927 for the play *In Abraham's Bosom.* He is credited with the concept of an outdoor theater. A close friend of Thomas Wolfe, Green was an honorary pallbearer at Wolfe's funeral in Asheville.

The theater is part of the Fort Raleigh National Historic site, which tells the story of the early settlers through exhibits and interpretive guides. Travelers can wander the beautiful Elizabethan Gardens, where azaleas, daffodils, and magnolias bloom in the springtime.

The Lost Colony, 1409 National Park Drive, Manteo, NC 27954

(252-473-3414; www.thelostcolony.org)

⑤ LITERARY LODGING

TRANQUIL HOUSE INN

Overlooking Shallowbag Bay, this lovely lodging spot is within easy reach of Roanoke Island Festival Park. The inn looks historic but was constructed in the 1980s. Custom cypress woodwork, beveled stained-glass windows, and four-poster beds enhance its appeal. Many of its 25 rooms come with bay views. A complimentary continental breakfast and evening wine and cheese are included in the room rate. Dining in the **1587 Restaurant** with picturesque views of the bay might be another highlight of your visit.

Tranquil House Inn, 405 Queen Elizabeth Avenue, Manteo, NC 27954 (252-473-1404; www.tranquilhouseinn.com)

⑧ EXCURSIONS AND DIVERSIONS

THE OUTER BANKS

Stretching 200 miles from the southern tip of Virginia to North Carolina is a barrier island abundant with wild dunes, lighthouses, and some of the prettiest beaches on the East Coast. Wild mustangs, descendants of horses that escaped from Spanish galleons, roam these shores and can often be spotted near the **Currituck Banks National Estuarine Research Reserve. The Whalehead Club**—just beyond the charming and intimate town of Duck—dates back to the 1920s and was built primarily as a hunting club. Today this park overlooking Currituck Sounds is a nature preserve where you might spot snowy egrets, great blue herons, and ospreys. (In fact, the Outer Banks has one of the largest populations of ospreys on the East Coast; nests are visible throughout the island.) **The Outer Banks Center for Wildlife Education,** also near Duck, has an informative exhibit on the area's bird and wildlife. Within walking distance of this is the **Currituck Lighthouse**—the northernmost lighthouse on the Outer Banks. Opened in 1875, it has been completely restored. If you are up to it, climb the 214 steps for a panoramic view of Currituck Sound.

　　Aviation history comes to life at the Outer Banks most visited attraction, the **Wright Brothers National Memorial at Kill Devil Hills,** a National Park Service site. Here you can see where history was made on December 17, 1903, when the brothers form Ohio took to the skies on their brief 20-foot climb. A film, exhibit area, and a striking white marble monument atop the windswept hill where Wilbur and Orville Wright flew can be enjoyed on a visit. The admission ticket is good for five consecutive days.

Farther down the road is one of the most unusual parks in the country. **Jockey Ridge State Park** is famous for having the highest sand dunes on the East Coast. Hang gliding, sand surfing, and kite flying are some of the activities you can enjoy in this spot. A visitors center has a small exhibit on the dunes and is across from where you can register to take hang-gliding lessons.

If you head to the **Cape Hatteras National Seashore,** before crossing the bridge visit the **Bodie Inlet Lighthouse.** One of the most photographed lighthouses in the world, the towering sentinel overlooks a boardwalk and marsh area that is prime birding habitat.

Outer Banks Visitors Bureau, I Visitors Center Circle, Manteo, NC 27954 (I-877-629-4386, www.outerbanks.org)

ᕬ Southern Pines

> He made his monuments, his tracks, cut his path, planted his trees by time's river—all to testify that he had passed this way.
> —PAUL GREEN, IN THE INTRODUCTION
> TO JAMES BOYD'S *Eighteen Poems*

DURING THE 1920S AND '30S Southern Pines,—a community in North Carolina's Sandhills region about an hour south of Raleigh—was a glamorous gathering place for writers and artists.

James Boyd, a Princeton graduate who wrote the Revolutionary War novel *Drums,* settled in the area in 1921. Boyd, who inherited the land from his grandfather, originally came to North Carolina from Pennsylvania. The gentleman scholar was an acquaintance of F. Scott Fitzgerald, Thomas Wolfe, and Max Perkins During World War II, Boyd collaborated with Archibald MacLeish, John Steinbeck, and Paul Green on radio plays. Boyd built the Georgian manor house named **Weymouth** as a private retreat.

Boyd was known for his lavish parties. When Thomas Wolfe—whom Boyd called "Gulliver"—arrived, he would usually climb into an open window and find the nearest couch to bunk down for the night. Fitzgerald and Wolfe usually became a little tipsy on their visits but Boyd, ever the congenial host, forgave his friends, knowing that their time at Weymouth provided them with a welcome respite from their cares and literary obligations. Fitzgerald traveled from Asheville and spent countless nights in the wooded enclave to escape Zelda's ongoing mental illness.

Since 1979 Weymouth has been a vibrant cultural center hosting seminars, literary readings, concerts, and cultural events. There is an annual chamber music series, along with the Blumenthal Writers and Readers Series.

Two of the upstairs rooms are named after Fitzgerald and Wolfe; the upstairs study is home to the North Carolina Writers Hall of Fame. The handsome oak-paneled room devotes its walls to North Carolina's most celebrated authors. Lining its walls are photographs of Thomas Wolfe, Paul Green, Reynolds Price, Sam Ragan, and William Sydney Porter (O. Henry). The house has been restored to reflect Boyd's era; the Poets Garden offers a peaceful hiking trail.

Weymouth Center for the Arts & Humanities, 555 East Connecticut Avenue, Southern Pines, NC 28387 (910-692-6261; www.weymouthcenter.org)

§ LITERARY LODGING

PINEHURST RESORT

Whispers of the past linger at the Pinehurst Resort. Situated just a few miles from James Boyd's Weymouth, it would not be surprising to discover that Fitzgerald made an appearance or two at this beautiful wooded property during his visits to Southern Pines.

Dubbed the "St. Andrews of America," Pinehurst has been associated with golfing greats for decades. Ben Hogan, Sam Snead, Arnold Palmer, Walter Hagan, and Bobby Jones have all strolled its hilly links in search of the perfect game. Its undulating fields of green and association with the great masters of the game add to

Pinehurst's nostalgic atmosphere and appeal.

Pinehurst was founded by New England millionaire James Tufts, of Tufts University fame, who made his fortune in the soda fountain business in Boston. Tufts traveled here to escape the dreary New England winters. In 1895 he purchased 5,000 acres of raw timberland and enlisted the architectural talents of Olmsted, Olmsted and Eliot (who also designed New York's Central Park) to carry out his plan.

The Holly Inn was the first cottage he built on the property. Resembling a Scottish tavern, the inn opened on New Year's Eve 1895; three dollars got you in the front door. Tufts's passion for golf whetted his appetite for more guests, greens, and rooms, and in 1901 he built the Carolina Inn on the property; it is often referred to as the "White House of Golf." In 1907 Donald Ross developed the course known as Pinehurst No. 2, and a golf legend was born.

Throughout the resort's history, celebrities and dignitaries have visited this peaceful enclave, which continues to exude Old World charm and elegance. Annie Oakley, John Philip Sousa, Mary Pickford, Douglas Fairbanks, and crooner Bing Crosby all traveled to this North Carolina hideaway. Presidents including Harding, Truman, and Ford have also frequented the retreat, as did Chief of Staff of the Army General George C. Marshall. In fact, Marshall purchased Liscombe Lodge in Pinehurst Village, and it is believed that he mapped out the Marshall Plan while living here. But golf lies at the heart of this historic hotel. The **Donald Ross Grill** is lined with photographs of golfing greats as well as trophies, with the course Pinehurst No. 2 as the site of the 1999 US Open. The **Ryder Cup Lounge** is located in the Carolina Inn. A spa and swimming pool are on site, and guests have access to bicycles for rides around Pinehurst Village.

Pinehurst Resort, 1 Carolina Vista Drive, Pinehurst, NC 28374 (910-235-8141; www.pinehurst.com)

✍ Southport

> *We were living at a place called Wrightsville Sound that spring, a most*
> *fascinating spot to be young in. It had numberless attractions for a boy.*
> *As is so much of the coastal South, it was semitropic. There were vast*
> *forests of gnarled, craggy live-oak trees, which were hung with Spanish*
> *moss, and tall timberlands of longleaf pine.*
>
> —ROBERT RUARK, *The Old Man and the Boy*

ROBERT RUARK AND MARILYN
KAYTOR IN PALAMOS, SPAIN, 1965.
Photo by Kevin C. Fitzpatrick. Wikimedia Commons, p.d.

THE LIFE COURSE OF ROBERT RUARK began
in Southport and ended halfway around the world
where he worked as a journalist and novelist. It was
a path with all the bravado, gusto, and enthusiasm
of Ernest Hemingway—whom Ruark considered
to be the finest writer who ever lived. Ruark's innate love of adventure took him to the four corners
of the globe, with Africa his favorite destination.
In his book *Something of Value*, he captures the soul
of the Dark Continent.

Ruark learned his craft as a journalist following his studies at the University of North
Carolina–Chapel Hill and in 1935 headed to
Washington, DC, where he found work as a copy boy and then reporter
for the *Washington Daily News* and the Scripps Howard News Service.

Ruark learned his appreciation for the outdoors during childhood
summers spent in Southport and along the North Carolina coast with his
grandfather. Nature is a theme in his early writings.

"If you are a very small boy," he wrote in *The Old Man and the Boy*,
"being close to the water makes the summer a marvelous thing. There is
something of the kiss of the sun on dancing little waves, fresh salt breeze
in your face and sun on your head, the taste of salt fresh on your lips. It
was like that this day when the Old Man taught me to use the cast net
and all the fish were hungry for the little gray shrimp we had caught on
the edges of steaming marshes."

But those wonderful coastal Carolina summers did not prevent the
ambitious writer from succumbing to the cirrhosis of the liver. He died
in London and is buried in Palamos, Spain.

🖋 LITERARY LODGING

THE ROBERT RUARK INN

THE ROBERT RUARK INN

The Robert Ruark Inn on Lord Street in the heart of Southport's historic district is the former home of Ruark's grandfather, Captain Adkins. Completely restored in 2009, this lovely yellow Victorian inn offers four rooms with one named after the author. This room evokes Ruark's love of Africa, while a sleigh bed, gas fireplace, and writing desk accent its literary ambience. A full southern breakfast offering River Pilot scrambled eggs, country ham, and blueberry pancakes is included in your room tariff. Bicycles are provided to guests for scooting around this lovely coastal North Carolina town.

Robert Ruark Inn, 119 North Lord Street, Southport, NC 28461 (910-363-4169; www.robertruarkinn.com)

⚙ EXCURSIONS AND DIVERSIONS

NORTH CAROLINA MARITIME MUSEUM

The North Carolina Maritime Museum in Southport highlights North Carolina's rich maritime heritage. Exhibits pertain to the history of the Cape Fear River and follow Civil War battles. You'll also find artifacts relating to the Colonial port of Brunswick. A self-guided walking tour available from the Southport Visitors Center travels along the historic port village.

North Carolina Maritime Museum, 204 East Moore Street, Southport, NC 28461; (910-457-0003; www.ncmaritime museums.com)

❧ Wilmington

Some of the happier days of my life were spent on the hometown beach.
It was called Wrightsville named for a local family, who were my best
friends.

—DAVID BRINKLEY, *A Memoir*

NORTH CAROLINA'S LARGEST COASTAL COMMUNITY is where journalist, correspondent, and broadcaster David Brinkley—most famous for his nightly news report with Chet Huntley—grew up and attended New Hanover High School (as did Southport native Robert Ruark). It was during Brinkley's high school years and under the influence of English teacher Mrs. Burrows Smith that he decided to become a writer. Attending the University of North Carolina–Chapel Hill, Brinkley honed his news writing skills before heading off to Washington to co-anchor *NBC Nightly News*. Following his broadcasting days he wrote a series of books including his *Memoir*.

The Brinkley family lived at **801 Princess Street,** now long gone. In his *Memoir* he wrote of living "in a vaguely Victorian house under the branches of an oak tree, older than our country, lying in bed at night listening to acorns bouncing and rattling on the red tin roof."

Brinkley frequently reminisced and remembered his Wilmington days long after he achieved national and international acclaim. Again in his *Memoir* he wrote, "Summer 1930. The Cape Fear River docks at the foot of Walnut Street in Wilmington, North Carolina. Clear. Warm. Sunny. Mark Twain would have found no romantic adventure here. No humor. Unlike his Mississippi River, the Cape Fear hardly went anywhere. . . . Beyond Wilmington, there was only shallow water and no room for Twain's steamboats, and their paddlewheel gamblers and fancy women."

Brinkley passed away in June 2003 and is interred at Wilmington's **Oakdale Cemetery.**

Oakdale Cemetery, 520 North 15th Street, Wilmington, NC 28401 (910-762-5682)

⚜ LITERARY LODGING

GREYSTONE INN

Conveniently located near the Cape Fear River and the historic district, the Greystone Inn is an AAA Four-Diamond property offering nine distinctly designed rooms; a full southern breakfast is included in the room rate. A parlor, dining room, veranda, and library are at your disposal at this Georgian mansion. A complimentary glass of wine is served in the library in the evenings, capping off a day of exploring Wilmington. The congenial hosts will recommend dining options and provide area information and suggestions as to what to see and do. Since Wilmington is second only to Hollywood in television and film production, many a Hollywood star has stayed at the Greystone Inn.

Greystone Inn, 100 South 3rd Street, Wilmington, NC 28401 (910-763-2000; www.greystoneinn.com)

⚙ EXCURSIONS AND DIVERSIONS

CAPE FEAR RIVER CRUISE

Taking a cruise on the Cape Fear River is a great way to experience the area that David Brinkley recalls in his *Memoir*. **Wilmington Water Tours** offers seasonal tours of the waterway. The Blackwater Adventure wanders through inlets and marshes where you might see alligators, river otters, and an abundance of bird life. You can also see the battleship USS *North Carolina* that was part of the Pacific Fleet during World War II on this tour.

Wilmington Water Tours, 212 South Water Street, Wilmington, NC 28401 (910-338-3134; www.wilmingtonwatertours.net)

Wilmington Beaches CVB, 505 Nutt Street, Unit A, Wilmington, NC 28401 (910-341-4030, 1-877-406-2356, www.wilmingtonandbeaches.com)

CHAPTER
8

$\mathcal{S}$OUTH CAROLINA

T HE FIRST OF THE SOUTHERN STATES to secede from the Union, South Carolina triggered one of the most tumultuous chapters in American history when the first shots of the Civil War were fired from Fort Sumter on April 12, 1861.

The Civil War and its aftermath destroyed much of Charleston's architecture but not the enduring spirit of its citizens. "Too poor to paint and too proud to whitewash" became their adopted slogan following the war.

Soft breezes along the Battery at dusk today engulf its historic district, where faint echoes of a more graceful and genteel way of life reverberate. The Low Country just beyond Charleston displays some of the most beautiful antebellum homes and plantations in the South, with hanging moss and live oaks. Naturalist John James Audubon navigated this terrain en route to Florida and captured its mystical loveliness in many of his bird paintings.

Charleston also became the setting for Dubose Heyward's poignant story *Porgy*, which composer George Gershwin put to music. It went on to become one of Broadway's most beloved musicals.

The state capital in Columbia is within reach of the Congaree National Park resplendent with what James Dickey must have envisioned when he wrote *Deliverance*. Edgar Allan Poe's name is associated with Charleston; he wrote "The Gold Bug" while stationed at Fort Moultrie. Pat Conroy and his *Prince of Tides* must also be mentioned, along with Josephine Humphries, whose novels including *Rich in Love*, depict southern themes and settings. John Jakes's trilogy *North and South* told stories of South Carolina . Matthew Bruccoli's exhaustive work on F. Scott Fitzgerald elevated his literary status at the University of South Carolina in Columbia.

From Charleston to Columbia, the Palmetto State has its own unique brand of writers. Meet them on a tour through this thoroughly enticing state.

ᐕ Charleston

> *They tell me that she is beautiful, my city,*
> *That she is colorful and quaint; alone*
> *Among the cities. But I—I who have known*
> *Her tenderness, her courage, and her pity;*
> *Have felt her forces mold me, mind and bone . . .*
> *How can I think of her in wood and stone!*
>
> —DuBose Heyward, "Dusk"

IF ANY SOUTHERN TOWN PERSONIFIES the uniqueness and irresistible appeal of the South, it's Charleston. It was here on April 12, 1861, that the first shots were fired at Fort Sumter, ushering in the four-year conflict between the North and the South known as the Civil War.

From the lushness of the Low Country to Charleston's priceless architectural treasures, earthquakes, hurricanes, and the tumult of the Civil War have not kept this utterly enticing state from flourishing and becoming one of the South's most popular and visited destinations. Pastel-colored dwellings reminiscent of the predominant West Indies influences define the city's historic section, where warm, caressing breezes from the confluences of the Ashley and Cooper Rivers engulf the Battery.

Perhaps because of its tormented and tragic past, writers have gravitated to the exotic landscape framed by palmetto trees and moss-strewn

RAINBOW ROW

live oaks. The cultivation of rice, indigo, and cotton created countless fortunes for many of its early settlers, who built grand estates like Middleton Place and Magnolia Plantation.

Take a walk along Church Street. Number 76 is where DuBose Heyward lived while writing the novel *Porgy*. Just around the corner on East Bay is Rainbow Row—a profusion of vibrantly colored row houses that became the inspiration for the book's Catfish Row. A small plaque beside the canary-yellow house commemorates *Porgy and Bess.* This is where Heyward set his story, which is now such an important part of Charleston's fabric.

Charleston native DuBose Heyward—born here in 1885—is perhaps Charleston's most celebrated author. His haunting story *Porgy* revealed Charleston's strong African American influences as well as its Gullah culture. While employed as a dockworker, Heyward listened to stories and observed the African Americans, basing Porgy on Sammy Small, a disabled man who got around Charleston in a goat cart. In fact, many of the characters in the book are based on actual individuals he observed. African American poet and playwright Langston Hughes described Heyward as one who saw "with his white eyes, wonderful, poetic qualities in the inhabitants of Catfish Row that makes them come alive."

The book, published in 1925, became an immediate hit and captured the attention of New York composer George Gershwin, who was given a copy as a gift. After reading it, he wrote to Heyward expressing his desire to transform the story into a folk opera. Gershwin believed that with all its passion, the enthralling tale was a natural for a musical adaptation blending blues with jazz. But Heyward's and Gershwin's creation would take years to take shape. The two men corresponded for several years before Heyward convinced Gershwin to come to Charleston to experience the pulse and tempo of the Gullah culture that permeates *Porgy and Bess.*

The summer of 1934 marked the beginning of their creative collaboration. Gershwin's arrival in Charleston was celebrated with a series of social functions where he met DuBose and Dorothy Heyward. The composer rented a small house in Folly Beach and had a piano delivered as he began his compositions for the musical. He immersed himself in the local culture, attending church to learn more about Gullah life and musical heritage. He often invited residents into his house and played and sang them a host of tunes. When not composing, he walked along the beach. He and Heyward worked tirelessly on the music, lyrics, and scenes of the play. Heyward wrote the lyrics for "Summertime" and "My Man's Gone Now," and both men quickly realized that their work was going to be groundbreaking. The entire summer was devoted to writing and rewriting the score.

At summer's end Gershwin headed back to New York to begin fine-tuning the musical that proved to be his most personal accomplishment. He completed 700 pages of music while Heyward scripted scenes for the musical. In a letter to Gershwin, Heyward wrote, "I find my creative ability practically paralyzed in a new environment. I am just getting into my stride here now, and I do not want to risk breaking it."

After several revisions by both Gershwin and Heyward, "Porgy and Bess" opened on Broadway on October 10, 1935 at the Alvin Theater to mixed reviews. The play closed after 124 performances and became a bitter heartbreak for both men who had worked so effortlessly on the show that had been such an important part of their lives.

The play opened on October 10, 1935, at New York's Alvin Theatre to mixed reviews and closed after 124 performances. It was a bitter disappointment for both men. Later on, of course, *Porgy and Bess* would gather momentum and become one of Broadway's most enduring hits. Just two years after its premiere on Broadway, Gershwin died from a brain tumor; in 1940 Heyward collapsed from a heart attack. Yet *Porgy and Bess* lives on in Charleston, where travelers still visit Rainbow Row. *The Sound of Charleston*, a concert series, presents music from gospel to Gershwin in the city's historic Congregational Church from June through December. Spirituals, Civil War camp songs, and Gershwin's beloved *Porgy and Bess* are performed by a talented ensemble.

The "Porgy Trail" begins in the historic district at **76 Church Street** off Meeting Street. Heyward lived in the house from 1919 until 1924, and this is where he wrote the majority of *Porgy*. There is a brass plaque commemorating his residence. The private residence is a National Historic Landmark and is near Rainbow Row. **St. Phillips Episcopal Church,** 142 Church Street, is where he is interred. You might just find yourself humming a few bars of "Summertime" as you immerse yourself in this literary destination.

South Carolina's Edgar Allan Poe Connection

Edgar Allan Poe, taking the assumed name Edgar A. Perry, was stationed at **Fort Moultrie** outside Charleston, near the tip of **Sullivan's Island,** beginning in 1827. The army private had traveled from Boston on the brigantine *Waltham;* his South Carolina adventure, though brief, left a lasting impression on the writer.

His short story "The Gold-Bug," published in 1843, is set on Sullivan's Island. In the story Poe describes it this way: "This island is a very singular one. It consists of little else than the sea sand, and is about three miles long. Its breadth at no point exceeds a quarter of a mile. It is separated from the mainland by a scarcely perceptible creek, oozing its way through a wilderness of reeds and slime, a favorite resort of the marshhen. The vegetation, as might be supposed, is scant, or at least dwarfish. No trees of any magnitude are to be seen. Near the western extremity, where Fort Moultrie stands, and where are some miserable frame buildings, tenanted, during summer, by the fugitives from Charleston dust and fever, may be found, indeed, the bristly palmetto; but the whole island, with the exception of this western point, and a line of hard, white beach on the sea-coast, is covered with a dense undergrowth of the sweet myrtle so much prized by the horticulturists of England. The shrub here often attains the height of fifteen or twenty feet, and forms an almost impenetrable coppice, burthening the air with its fragrance."

Poe reminders are found throughout the island, from the street names **Poe Avenue, Goldbug Avenue,** and **Raven Drive** to the local library, also named after Poe. The librarians here are well versed on Sullivan's most famous literary resident and will gladly direct you to Fort Moultrie, now managed by the US National Park Service, and to the local watering hole **Poe's Tavern.** Many of the locals confirm that on certain moonlit evenings, a black raven can be seen hovering above Fort Moultrie.

Edgar Allan Poe Library, 1921 L'On Avenue, Sullivan's Island, SC 29482 (843-883-3914; www.sullivansisland-sc.com/poe library.aspx)

Fort Moultrie, 1214 Middle Street, Sullivan's Island, SC 29482 (843-883-3123; www.nps.gov/fosu/historyculture/fort_ moultrie.htm)

Poe's Tavern, 2210 Middle Street, Sullivan's Island, SC 29482 (843-883-0083; www.poestavern.com)

LITERARY LODGING

HISTORIC DISTRICT INNS

In Charleston—one of America's most historic towns—you can choose from a host of vintage and intimate inns and grand hotels, most within walking distance of the Battery and historic district.

The **Kings Courtyard Inn** and the **John Rutledge House Inn** are both situated in the historic district. The John Rutledge House dates to 1763; Rutledge himself, one of the nation's founding fathers, wrote several drafts of the US Constitution on its second floor. It now offers two thoroughly charming carriage houses. Ironwork, marble fireplaces, and inlaid floors accentuate the lovely interiors. Built in 1853, the Kings Courtyard is a Greek Revival design and one of Charleston's most historic landmarks. Both of these inns offer complimentary breakfasts, parking, and concierge service.

Kings Courtyard Inn, 198 King Street, Charleston, SC 29401 (1-800-845-6119; www.kingscourtyardinn.com)

John Rutledge House Inn, 116 Broad Street, Charleston, SC 29401 (1-800-476-9741; www.johnrutledgehouseinn.com)

CHARLESTON HIGHLIGHTS

Fort Sumter is a must for any student of history on a swing through Charleston. The federal fort was constructed following the War of 1812 and is where the first shots of the Civil War were fired in April 1861. The fort is accessible by boat from either Patriot's Point in Mount Pleasant or the Fort Sumter Visitors Education Center in downtown Charleston.

Touring the historic district—either via horse-drawn carriage or on a walking tour—is highly recommended. **Plantation Row** is just a few miles from town along the Ashley River Road. An arched canopy of live oaks and hanging Spanish moss leads you to several plantations that really showcase Charleston's Old South lineage and many of its families. **Drayton Hall, Magnolia Place,** and **Middleton Place** are all found along this famed thoroughfare, with the latter by far the most interesting to visit. Middleton Place was burned during the Civil War, but luckily for visitors today part of the brick structure has survived. A National Historic Landmark, Middleton Place is situated on 65 acres including sculpted terraces, parterres, and reflecting pools; in spring pink azaleas accent the setting.

Roughly an hour from Charleston, depending on traffic, is **Kiawah Island Golf Resort.** Designated an **Audubon refuge,** Kiawah is privately owned but open to the public for lodging, nature excursions, golf, and tennis. The real attraction, however, is the scenery on the 10-mile-long resort island, which exemplifies South Carolina's Low Country beauty. Maritime forests, tidal creeks, and freshwater ponds here are home to bobcats, river otters, oystercatchers, avocets, and black-bellied plovers. You can also find loggerhead turtles and more than 600 alligators inhabiting its freshwater ponds.

Middleton Place, 4300 Ashley River Road, Charleston, SC 29414 (1-800-782-3608; www.middletonplace.org)

Kiawah Island Golf Resort, 1 Sanctuary Beach Drive, Kiawah Island, SC 29455 (1-800-654-2924; www.kiawahresort.com)

Charleston CVB, 423 King Street, Charleston, SC 29403 (843-853-8000, www.charlestoncvb.com)

ᏒᏎ Columbia

I came to poetry with no particular qualifications. I had begun to suspect,
however, that there is a poet—or a kind of poet—buried in every human
being like Arial in his tree, and that the people whom we are pleased to
call poets are only those who have felt the need and contrived the means
to release this spirit from its prison.

—JAMES DICKEY

SOUTH CAROLINA'S CAPITAL CITY is home to the main campus of
the University of South Carolina, where James Dickey served as poet in
residence from 1969 until his death in 1997. Born in Atlanta and educated
at Vanderbilt, Dickey wrote both poetry and fiction. His 1965 collection
Buckdancer's Choice won the National Book Award for Poetry. His novel *Deliverance* brought him widespread fame after a film version was released in
1972; Dickey wrote the screenplay.

His love of poetry began when he read Lord Byron. A graduate of
Vanderbilt University, Dickey referred to poetry as "language itself . . . a
miraculous medium which makes everything else that man has ever done
possible."

The James Dickey Library in the University of South Carolina's
Thomas Cooper Library houses Dickey's personal book collection for
the use of scholars and students. **The James Dickey Poetry Seminar
Room** on the mezzanine level of the library displays photographs and
personal items from Dickey's career.

Thomas Cooper Library, University of South Carolina, Columbia SC 29205 (803-777-3847; http://library.sc.edu)

DEAN OF FITZGERALD STUDIES

The University of South Carolina was the longtime intellectual home of
Matthew Bruccoli, the leading authority on Jazz Age author F. Scott
Fitzgerald and other literary figures including Ernest Hemingway and
Thomas Wolfe. Bruccoli launched the *Dictionary of Literary Biography*
and served as its editor. His biography of Fitzgerald, *Some Sort of Epic
Grandeur: The Life of F. Scott Fitzgerald,* was published in 1981. A

2008 obituary in the New York Times describes Bruccoli as the "dean of Fitzgerald Studies."

Bruccoli taught at USC for nearly 40 years and significantly increased the Thomas Cooper Library's Special Collections holdings on Fitzgerald.

---

§ LITERARY LODGING

THE INN AT CLAUSSENS

This inn is housed in a historic building dating back to 1928 and the former home of Claussens Bakery—a Columbia landmark. It's listed on the National Register of Historic Places. No two rooms are alike in this boutique inn that is near the University of South Carolina campus and all downtown sites. Hardwood floors, four-poster iron or brass beds with both traditional and contemporary furnishings, and loft suites with ascending staircases make this inn one of Columbia's most unusual. A complimentary breakfast is brought to your room; wine and cheese are offered during the evening hours.

The Inn at Claussens, 2003 Greene Street, Columbia, SC 29205 (803-765-0440 or 1-800-622-3382; www.theinnatclaussens .com)

⊕ EXCURSIONS AND DIVERSIONS

DELIVERANCE COUNTRY

Twenty-four miles from Columbia is the **Congaree National Park**—the largest tract of bottomland hardwood forest in the United States. Images of James Dickey's *Deliverance* quickly come to mind as you navigate this primeval wilderness setting. Kayaking, canoeing, and hiking are just some of the activities you can enjoy in this primitive terrain. Twenty-five miles of hiking trails are available, as are kayaking and canoe treks.

The park offers guided canoe trips on Cedar Creek by reservation throughout the year. (The canoes are provided for tours only.) These trips lead you through a watery wilderness of large bald cypress trees draped in Spanish moss. The sounds of the forest surround you, with songbirds, owls, and woodpeckers leading the way.

Be on the lookout for other wildlife along the riverbanks, including white-tailed deer, otters, and raccoons.

Another recommended paddling route is the **Congaree River Blue Trail**—a 50-mile recreational paddling trail that extends from the state capital in Columbia downstream to the Congaree National Park. This journey encompasses high bluffs, sandbars, and floodplain habitats.

Congaree National Park, 100 National Park Road, Hopkins, SC 29061 (803-783-4241; www.npca.org)

Ꮼ McClellanville

SOUTH CAROLINA'S FORMER POET LAUREATE Archibald Rutledge lived at the **Hampton Plantation.** This 322-acre property, a former rice plantation, is now a state park and wildlife habitat named in honor of Rutledge. This forested wilderness is among the state's most intriguing landscapes. Two prime wildlife areas, the Cape Romain National Wildlife Refuge and the Santee Coastal Reserve, are located nearby.

Hampton Plantation State Historic Site, 1950 Rutledge Road, McClellanville, SC 29458 (843-546-9361; www.southcarolina parks/hampton)

CHAPTER
9

TENNESSEE

THE NATCHEZ TRACE, the Great Smoky Mountains, country music, the blues, Memphis, Nashville, Knoxville . . . Tennessee lies at the intersection of *interesting* and *diverse*.

Music is at the heart of Nashville's character. Chances are nearly every gospel, country, bluegrass, rhythm-and-blues, and rock-and-roll star has at one time or another passed through Tennessee. Its diverse geography, encompassing forests, lakes, and mountains reflect the many personalities who have called it home—Andrew Jackson and Davy Crockett are perhaps its most celebrated and revered native sons. Its frontier spirit remains today.

The Volunteer State, so named because of the number of volunteers who signed on during the War of 1812, has also witnessed its fair share of darker moments. Battles in and near Shiloh, Chickamauga, and Chattanooga are painful chapters of its Civil War past.

Among the authors who borrowed from their Tennessee memories when penning their works are the Fugitives, a scholarly band of literary fellows at Vanderbilt University; Arna Bontemps, a member of the Harlem Renaissance; John Grisham, who cut his literary teeth in Memphis; and Alex Haley, the author who gave us *Roots*. James Agee of Knoxville and Peter Taylor of Trenton both won Pulitzer Prizes for their luminous stories.

Wherever you roam in this hilly and magnificently mountainous terrain, the clear voices and distant dreams of many Tennessee authors will surely surface.

ᔕ Henning

In all of us there is a hunger, marrow-deep, to know our heritage—to know who we are and where we have come from. Without this enriching knowledge, there is a hollow yearning. No matter what our attainments in life, there is still a vacuum, an emptiness, and the most disquieting loneliness.

—ALEX HALEY

AN HOUR'S DRIVE FROM MEMPHIS is the town of Henning, where African American author Alex Haley lived with his grandparents at 200 South Church Street, a 10-room bungalow in the center of town.

Best known for his book *Roots: The Saga of an American Family,* Haley listened to stories from his grandparents Will and Cynthia Palmer that would later find their way into his masterwork. By delving into his family's history, Haley pieced together a fascinating American tale. The story of Kunte Kinte and his family became the centerpiece of the novel that won a Pulitzer Special Citation in 1977. The book was an immediate bestseller and was later turned into a mini-series that became one of the most watched in television history.

The house, listed on the National Register of Historic Places, is devoted to Haley's life as a writer. Memorabilia, photographs, and family history fill an interior that recalls characters from *Roots.* A short video on the author's life and literary aspirations is available. Haley, a lifelong Tennessean, is interred on the property. The museum offers tours, special seminars throughout the year, and programs for children to keep his literary legacy alive.

Alex Haley Museum and Interpretive Center, 200 South Church Street, Henning, TN 38041 (731-738-2240; www.alexhaley museum.com)

ᒡ Knoxville

> *We are talking now of summer evenings in Knoxville, Tennessee, in the
> time that I lived there so successfully disguised to myself as a child. . . .
> It is of these evenings, I speak. Supper was at six and was over by half
> past. There was still daylight, shining softly and with a tarnish, like the
> lining of a shell.*
>
> —JAMES AGEE, *A Death in the Family*

IN THE HEART OF THE TENNESSEE VALLEY, midway between
Asheville and Louisville, is Knoxville—urban gateway to the Great Smoky
Mountains. The meandering Mississippi River cuts a swath through the
downtown district.

Home to the 400-acre University of Tennessee, Knoxville is the
hometown of James Agee—screenwriter, journalist, novelist, poet, and
film critic. The multi-talented writer described his life here in *A Death in
the Family*, published posthumously and awarded the Pulitzer Prize in 1958.
In the novel he recounted his Tennessee beginnings: "It was a little bit
mixed sort of block, fairly solidly lower middle class, with one or two juts
apiece on either side of that. The houses corresponded: middle-sized
gracefully fretted wood houses built in the late nineties and early nineteen
hundreds, with small front and side and more spacious back yards and
trees in the yards, and porches. . . . There were fences around one or two
of the two houses, but mainly the yards ran into each other with only now
and then a low hedge that wasn't doing very well."

Agee's youth was marked with tragedy when his father was killed
in an automobile accident; he was six years old. That great loss pro-
foundly affected his writing, finding its way onto the pages of *A Death
in the Family*. Educated at Saint Andrews School in Sewanee, Agee became
close friends with Father James Flye, who became a lifelong friend and
mentor. He attended Knoxville High School in 1924 and then transferred to Exeter Academy in New Hampshire, where he was editor of
the *Exeter Monthly*. In his correspondence with Flye he mentioned his love
of literature and reading and added, "I have written stuff for the
Monthly, and I am to get a story and 2 or 3 poems in this month. This
will get me into the Lantern Club, I hope. . . . It gets several authors up
each term who give very informal talks in the club room. Booth Tark-

ington, who graduated here, came several times, and Sinclair Lewis may come this winter."

Following Exeter, Agee continued his studies at Harvard University, where he was editor in chief of the *Harvard Advocate*. Upon graduation the Tennessee author snapped up a $25-per-week job at *Time* magazine. Though he may be best known for his screenplays for *The African Queen* and Stephen Crane's *The Bride Comes to Yellow Sky*, Agee's haunting story of his childhood in Tennessee and recollections of the loss of a parent have made *A Death in the Family* his most widely read and acclaimed work. *Let Us Now Praise Famous Men*—his collaboration with photographer Walker Evans on Alabama sharecroppers—also received critical acclaim.

On the University of Tennessee campus is Fort Sanders, where an arbor, magnolias, and a walking trail comprise **James Agee Park,** dedicated in 2003. At the southeastern entrance is where you will find one of his most poignant quotes: "To those who in all times have sought truth and who have told it in their art or in their living."

At the corner of James Agee Street and Cumberland Avenue is a Tennessee Historical Marker that pays tribute to the author. This site was the location of his boyhood home, which was demolished in 1962 to make way for an apartment building.

More Knoxville Literary Highlights

The **Hodges Library** at the **University of Tennessee** has private collections of James Agee, along with Alex Haley and novelist David Madden. Cormac McCarthy briefly wrote for the university's literary magazine. Winner of both a National Book Award and a Pulitzer Prize, McCarthy's celebrated novels include *No Country for Old Men* (2005); he's written nearly a dozen others.

Other literary stops in Knoxville include the statue of Alex Haley in **Alex Haley Heritage Square,** part of Morningside Park in East Knoxville. The writer best known for tracing ancestry and *Roots* is remembered by a 13-foot bronze statue of him reading a book; it is the centerpiece of the square, named in February 1998 during Black History Month.

The **Clarence Brown Theatre** on the campus of the University of Tennessee is also worth a visit. Brown was a highly respected film director responsible for such movies as *The Yearling, National Velvet, Intruder in the Dust,* and *Anna Karenina*. He is memorialized at the university's performing arts center—considered one of the finest on any university campus.

Hodges Library, University of Tennessee, 1015 Volunteer Boulevard, Knoxville, TN 37996 (865-974-4351; www.lib.utk.edu /aboutlibs/hodges)

Clarence Brown Theatre, University of Tennessee, 1714 Andy Holt Avenue, Knoxville, TN 37916 (865-974-4867; www .clarencebrowntheatre.com)

🍷 LITERARY LODGING

THE OLIVER HOTEL

This boutique hotel on Market Square in the heart of Knoxville dates back to 1876, when it was the Peter Kern Bakery. All of its 28 rooms display original artworks and handcrafted furniture. Plush and comfy down duvets, amenities by Gilchrest & Soames, and a cozy lobby setting make the Oliver one of Knoxville's most popular accommodations. The Peter Kern Library is an ideal place for a special meeting and a glass of wine.

The Oliver Hotel, 407 Union Avenue, Knoxville, TN 39702 (865-521-0050; www.theoliverhotel.com)

🌐 EXCURSIONS AND DIVERSIONS

CRESCENT BEND HOUSE & GARDENS

Crescent Bend is a 600-acre farm west of the city. Its Armstrong-Lockett House recalls the 18th century with antiques and period furniture. And the formal Italian gardens are some of the most breathtaking in the South. Terraces and five fountains make this the city's botanical showplace. During the Civil War the house was occupied by both Union soldiers and Confederates, who camped out inside prior to Federal occupation.

Crescent Bend House & Gardens, 2728 Kingston Pike, Knoxville, TN 37919 (865-637-3163; www.crescentbend.com)

Visit Knoxville, 301 South Gay Street, Knoxville, TN 37902 (1-800-727-8045, www.knoxville.org)

✎ Memphis

The five-story building had been built a hundred years earlier by a cotton merchant and his sons after the Reconstruction, during the revival of cotton trading in Memphis. . . . Deserted, neglected, then renovated time and again since the first war, it had been purchased for good in 1951 by an aggressive tax lawyer named Anthony Bendini. He renovated it yet again and began filling it with lawyers. He renamed it the Bendini Building.

—JOHN GRISHAM, *The Firm*

WHILE MUSIC IS THE BEATING HEART of Memphis—what with Beale Street being the birthplace of the blues, and the Elvis phenomenon at Graceland—the city's intriguing history also includes tales of riverboat gamblers and rich cotton brokers, making it a natural canvas for writers and stories.

This city overlooking the Mississippi is endowed with impressive literary sons and daughters, most notably Peter Taylor (*A Summons to Memphis*), Shelby Foote (*Shiloh*), and lawyer-turned-author John Grisham, who has used the Tennessee town in many of his bestselling novels, including *The Rainmaker, The Client,* and *The Firm*—his first commercial success set entirely in Memphis.

The Grisham connections are easy to find. His affection for Memphis began while he was a student at Mississippi State and Ole Miss Law School. A native of Jonesboro, Arkansas, Grisham practiced law in Southaven, Mississippi, before turning legal briefs into first drafts. His collection of bestselling novels quickly separated him from the lawyer literary pack. No backwoods southern lawyer, he continues to churn out legal thrillers and novels. *The Firm,* based on a Memphis law firm, clearly elevated him to another level and made Memphis his literary home base.

But his eventual success did not come easily. When he first began his literary journey, rejections came in almost daily. Still, he never considered quitting what he loved to do best. In an interview with Mississippi State, Grisham elaborated on his perseverance: "I never thought of quitting. My attitude was: 'What the heck, let's have some fun.' Honestly, I believe I would've sent it to several hundred people before I would have even thought of giving up." He continued, "I have had readers say they liked

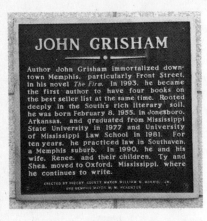

JOHN GRISHAM

Author John Grisham immortalized downtown Memphis, particularly Front Street, in his novel *The Firm*. In 1993, he became the first author to have four books on the best seller list at the same time. Rooted deeply in the South's rich literary soil, he was born February 8, 1955, in Jonesboro, Arkansas, and graduated from Mississippi State University in 1977 and University of Mississippi Law School in 1981. For ten years, he practiced law in Southaven, a Memphis suburb. In 1990, he and his wife, Renee, and their children, Ty and Shea, moved to Oxford, Mississippi, where he continues to write.

ERECTED BY SHELBY COUNTY MAYOR WILLIAM N. MORRIS, JR.
AND MEMPHIS MAYOR W. W. HERENTON

the book because 'it really flowed.' As a writer that is a tremendous compliment, because it is truly painful to write smoothly."

He has also been quoting as saying, "I seriously doubt I would ever have written the first story had I not been a lawyer. I never dreamed of being a writer. I wrote only after witnessing a trial."

Many Grisham sites from *The Firm* are visible in Memphis. **The Cotton Exchange Building** at 65 Union Avenue is the most obvious. Here a small brass plaque at the entrance pays tribute to the city's favorite literary son with a brief biography. The Cotton Exchange Building is also one of the city's most revered and important architectural landmarks and has, since 2006, hosted a museum devoted to cotton. Memphis is the largest spot-cotton market in the world, and within the museum you can take in video footage, oral histories, and exhibits that tell the story of King Cotton.

Confederate Park at Jefferson and Front Streets was the location for secret meetings between Mitch McDeere and Eddie Lomax in *The Firm*. Beale Street and Mud Island also featured in the novel. (See the Mississippi chapter for information on Grisham connections in that state.)

The Cotton Museum at the Memphis Cotton Exchange, 65 Union Avenue, Memphis TN 38103 (901-531-7826; www .memphiscottonmuseum.org)

SHELBY FOOTE

Shelby Foote, the renowned historian responsible for writing a series of Civil War histories and biographies, lived much of his life in Memphis. Born in Greenville, Mississippi, Foote is interred at **Elmwood Cemetery,** one of Memphis's oldest. He is buried under an old magnolia tree with a simple marker stating his name, date of birth, and date of death.

Elmwood Cemetery, 824 South Dudley Street, Memphis, TN 38104 (901-774-3212; www.elmwoodcemetery.org)

◊ LITERARY LODGING

THE PEABODY HOTEL

The Peabody Hotel is one of the South's grandest. To quote author-historian David Cohn, "The Mississippi Delta begins in the lobby of the Peabody Hotel and ends on Catfish Row in Vicksburg." John Grisham and William Faulkner are among the literary figures associated with the hotel, with William Faulkner having a suite named in his honor.

The city's most noted lodging address is named after Memphis businessman George Peabody and dates back to the post–Civil War period; it's listed on the National Register of Historic Places. Situated in the heart of Memphis, the hotel is responsible for revitalizing the downtown. Being on the back door of Beale Street makes this hotel not only the most

LOBBY OF THE PEABODY HOTEL
Courtesy of The Peabody Memphis

luxurious in the city but also the most happening. Jazz clubs and rib joints are just outside its door. William Faulkner would drive up from Oxford, Mississippi, to buy his Dunhill pipe tobacco in the hotel and sit in the lobby to observe the comings and goings of guests. The Belz family of Memphis is responsible for bringing back this grand lady of the south—and yes, those adorable mallard ducks, the Peabody's trademark, still waddle through the lobby fountain at noon, making them the most popular stars in town.

The Peabody Memphis, 149 Union Avenue, Memphis, TN 38103 (901-529-4000; www.peabodymemphis.com)

Memphis CVB, 47 Union Avenue, Memphis, TN 38103 (901-543-5300, www.memphistravel.com)

ᔥ Nashville

I carry the old Nashville in my head, grateful for the friends it gave me and for so much else. . . . I have often thought that for me and my purposes and aspirations, it was the best place in the world. I couldn't want it to have been any different than what it was.

—ROBERT PENN WARREN,
QUOTED IN *Nashville* BY JOHN EGERTON

REGARDED AS THE "ATHENS OF THE SOUTH," Nashville may be best known for the country music industry—but its two universities, have had major importance in two of America's trendsetting literary movements. Vanderbilt University had its Fugitives, a band of writers who created a new voice for southern literature. Fisk University, meanwhile, was strongly connected to the Harlem Renaissance. The city also hosts the Southern Festival of the Book—one of the South's premier book festivals, staged in downtown Nashville. All this makes Nashville a very relevant literary destination.

The city is also a major publishing center. In the 1920s and '30s Vanderbilt's Ivy League atmosphere attracted a host of southern writers who wrote for *The Fugitive* magazine, including John Crowe Ransom, Allen Tate, Laura Riding Jackson, and Robert Penn Warren—the group's most celebrated poet and author.

Warren, who enrolled at Vanderbilt at 16, had plans to attend the US Naval Academy in Annapolis, but an eye injury precluded this. His freshman English teacher at Vanderbilt, John Crowe Ransom, helped convince Warren to pursue a literary career. Of his mentor, Warren said, "He was a real live poet, in pants and vest, who had published a book and also fought in the war."

Reflecting on his life, Warren said, "I didn't expect to become a writer. My ambition was to be a naval officer and I got an appointment to Annapolis. Then I had an accident to my eyes—and then I went to Vanderbilt instead and started out in life as a chemical engineer. That didn't last but three weeks or so because I found the English courses so much more interesting."

The Kentucky author is remembered and honored at the **Robert Penn Warren Center for the Humanities** on the Vanderbilt campus. The handsome Victorian building is where the writer would often sit on the porch and read. Today scholars at Vanderbilt gather there and talk about various subjects pertaining to the humanities. He is also remembered at the **Jean and Alexander Heard Library's Jesse E. Wills Fugitive/Agrarian Collection.** The attractive room focuses on the school's most revered writers through photographs, books, news clippings, and sculptures of the famous literary band of brothers (and one sister). It houses the most comprehensive collection on the Fugitives and their writings in the country. William Faulkner is also represented in the room, as is Peter Taylor, who endowed a large portion of his papers to Vanderbilt.

Sportswriter Grantland Rice's name should also be added to university's roster. A former football player at Vanderbilt, Rice went on to write for the *New York Herald Tribune*, where he became known as the "Dean of American Sportswriters."

Fisk University is strongly associated with the Harlem Renaissance largely thanks to Arna Bontemps, the school's library director from 1943 until 1965. Because of Bontemps's arduous efforts—and his close friendship with poet Langston Hughes—Fisk's library houses one of the world's most esteemed collections of the Harlem Renaissance. "The Southern Negro's link with his past," Bontemps wrote of his African American heritage, "seems to me worth preserving. His greater pride in being himself, I would say, is all to the good, and I think I detect a growing nostalgia for these virtues." Fisk's Special Collections houses extensive papers of Langston Hughes, W. E. B. Du Bois, Scott Joplin, and George Gershwin, mostly as a result of Bontemps's curatorial and research expertise.

Robert Penn Warren Center for the Humanities, Vanderbilt University, 2301 Vanderbilt Place, Nashville, TN 37235 (615-343-6060; www.vanderbilt.edu/rpw_center)

Jean and Alexander Heard Library, Vanderbilt University, 419 21st Avenue South, Nashville, TN 37203 (615-322-7100; www.library.vanderbilt.edu)

Fisk University Library, 1000 17th Avenue North, Nashville, TN 37208 (615-329-8500; www.fisk.edu/academics/Library/SpecialCollections.aspx)

♫ LITERARY LODGING

NASHVILLE'S LODGING LEGENDS

Nashville is fortunate enough to have two legendary hotels—The Hermitage and Union Station Hotel—both located in the downtown area.

The Hermitage is owned by the same company that operates Richmond's AAA Five-Star Jefferson Hotel (see the Virginia chapter). Opened in 1910, the Hermitage can lay claim to being the first grand hotel in the city. The Beaux-Arts structure served as the headquarters for the Suffragette Movement in 1920 and has hosted everyone from cowboy star Gene Autry to several US presidents, bestselling authors, and Hollywood stars.

The hotel's lobby with its stained-glass windows is one of its most outstanding architectural features. Closed for several years, the hotel reopened to great fanfare on Valentine's Day 2003 following a $19 million renovation. Afternoon tea, concierge service, and the **Capital Grille** have made the 122-room hotel a Nashville favorite.

The Union Station Hotel, dating to 1900, served as Nashville's main railroad depot during the days of the Fugitives. The Romanesque-style design features barrel-vaulted ceilings decorated with 128 panels of multicolored stained glass and bas-relief sculptures. Opened in 1986 as a hotel, each of its 125 guest rooms offers individual decor and marble bathrooms. The Country Music Hall of Fame and Vanderbilt University are within easy walking distance of this historic landmark. Its fine dining spot, **Prime 108,** has dark walnut paneling, stained-glass windows, lunch banquettes, and a 1900 stone fireplace.

The Hermitage Hotel, 231 6th Avenue North, Nashville, TN 37219 (1-888-888-9414; www.thehermitagehotel.com)

Union Station Hotel, 1001 Broadway, Nashville, TN 37203 (615-726-1001; www.unionstationhotelnashville.com)

⚙ EXCURSIONS AND DIVERSIONS

MUSIC CITY AND MORE

Nashville serves up a host of activities and sites, with the **Country Music Hall of Fame and Museum** leading the list. Hank Williams,

Patsy Cline, Loretta Lynn, and Johnny Cash are remembered at this venue. Reopened in 2001, the $37 million facility is just south of the **Sommer Center.** The museum's playful exterior is reminiscent of a Cadillac fin, a piano, and a radio tower. Plaques, photographs, gold and platinum records, and a theater that shows a brief film on the industry make this museum a must for music enthusiasts.

Another stop for music aficionados is the **Ryman Auditorium**—known as the "Mother Church of Country Music"—which was home to the Grand Ole Opry from 1943 to 1974. Classical, pop, jazz, gospel and country music performers have graced the stages of this National Historic Landmark.

The **Tennessee State Capitol** and **Bicentennial Capitol Mall State Park** are two downtown sites that bring Tennessee's history to life. The **Tennessee Performing Arts Center** is also part of the complex, as is the **Frist Center for the Visual Arts**—the city's art gallery—which houses a children's discovery gallery, a café, and a gift shop.

Belle Meade Plantation, referred to as the "Queen of the Tennessee Plantations," is a Greek Revival house just outside Nashville that displays bullet holes in its columns from the Civil War. The 5,300-acre estate was one of the country's first thoroughbred breeding farms. Tours are led by costumed guides. Martha's at the Plantation is an ideal respite from sightseeing offering delectable southern cuisine.

Andrew Jackson is perhaps Tennessee's most interesting historical figure, and **the Hermitage,** 12 miles east of Nashville, is the house that "Old Hickory" built for his wife, Rachel. The 28,000-square-foot museum, visitors center, and education center tell the enthralling Jackson story. Allow at least four hours for exploring the house and gardens. You can see a film on Jackson at the visitors center and tour the mansion with guides. Both Jackson and his wife are interred at the Hermitage.

For seeing the beauty of the Cumberland River, a boat tour from downtown Nashville is recommended. You can view some of the palatial homes of country music stars that outline the riverfront. Tours are also available out to **Gaylord Opryland Resort**—a dining and entertainment complex just outside the city. This massive entertainment complex has indoor gardens, several restaurants, and the city's largest hotel—3,000 rooms.

Another option is the **Cheekwood Botanical Gardens and Museum of Art.** These 32 acres of gardens, carpeted with wildflowers, are home to a neo-Georgian mansion exhibiting American art until 1945, rotating exhibits, and Fabergé eggs.

Country Music Hall of Fame and Museum, 222 5th Avenue South, Nashville, TN 37203 (615-416-2001; http://country musichalloffame.org)

Ryman Auditorium, 116 5th Avenue North, Nashville, TN 37219 (615-889-3060; www.ryman.com)

Belle Mead Plantation, 5025 Harding Pike, Nashville, TN 37205 (1-800-270-3991; http://bellemeadeplantation.com)

The Hermitage, 4580 Rachel's Lane, Nashville, TN 37076 (615-889-2941; www.thehermitage.com)

Gaylord Opryland Resort & Convention Center, 2800 Opryland Drive, Nashville, TN 37214 (615-889-1000; www .marriott.com/hotels/travel/bnago-gaylord-opryland-resort-and-convention-center)

Cheekwood Botanical Gardens and Museum of Art, 1200 Forrest Park Drive, Nashville TN 37205 (615-356-8000; www.cheekwood.org)

Nashville CVB, One Nashville Place, 150 4th Avenue North, Suite G-250, Nashville, TN 37219 (615-259-4730, www.visit musiccity.com)

ᴄ᷎ Sewanee: The University of the South

We shall say only the leaves whispering
In the improbable mist of nightfall
That flies on multiple wing:
Night is the beginning and the end
　　　　　—ALLEN TATE, "ODE TO THE CONFEDERATE DEAD"

THE SPRAWLING 13,000-ACRE CAMPUS of the University of the South—known as the Domain—is one of the South's most beautiful. Modeled after Oxford and Cambridge, it is also home to the nation's oldest continuously published literary review, *The Sewanee Review.* The by-lines that have graced its pages include Flannery O'Connor, Robert Penn Warren, Hart Crane, Cormac McCarthy, and James Dickey. Located atop the Cumberland Plateau, the area's geographic beauty is astounding. Sewanee is also the location of St. Andrews School–Sewanee, attended by James Agee.

Tennessee Williams left his estate to the university because his maternal grandfather, Walter Dakin, was an 1895 graduate of the School of Theology. Williams directed in his will that a fund be established to foster and encourage creative writing. As a result of his generosity, the **Sewanee Writers' Conference** held each summer awards several Tennessee Williams Fellowships. (Williams's name is also attached to the **Tennessee Williams Performing Arts Center,** constructed in 1998.) The Writers' Conference, in existence for well over two decades, also has awards associated with other major Sewanee-affiliated writers including Conrad Aiken, whose younger brother established the Aiken-Taylor award. Writers Peter Taylor, Allen Tate, and Andrew Lytle are buried in the university cemetery.

Searching out the university's fictional connections is a fascinating process. In William Faulkner's *The Sound and the Fury,* Sewanee is the alma mater of Quentin Compson's father. Walker Percy's *Lost in the Cosmos* mentions the Lost Cove. Walker's cousin, William Alexander Percy, taught English at Sewanee and attended the school from 1900 until 1904. He, too, mentions the school and its scenic landscape in his work *Lanterns on the Levee.*

Sewanee: The University of the South, 735 University Avenue, Sewanee, TN 37383 (931-598-1223; www.sewanee.edu)

Sewanee Writers' Conference (http://sewaneewriters.org)

ⓢ LITERARY LODGING

EDGEWOOD INN BED & BREAKFAST
The Edgewood Inn Bed & Breakfast in Monteagle, a short distance from Sewanee, is a favorite for graduates attending alumni events or for travelers hoping to experience a quaint village inn and bucolic college setting all in one outing. Monteagle is one of Tennessee's most charming destinations, reminiscent of a New England village. The village was established over 100 years ago; historic wooden cottages still dot its landscape. Seven rooms and three suites are offered to guests; the Treehouse Suite is a particular favorite with writers with its garret-angled walls and skylights. The inn is located 45 miles northwest of Chattanooga and 85 miles southeast of Nashville.

The Edgeworth Inn Bed & Breakfast, 19 Wilkins Avenue, Monteagle, TN 37356 (931-924-4000; www.edgeworthinn.com)

ⓔ EXCURSIONS AND DIVERSIONS

SOUTH CUMBERLAND STATE RECREATION AREA
The South Cumberland State Recreation Area comprises more thab 300 acres of woodlands and features the Great Stone Door, Lost Cove Cave, Cathedral Falls, and Fiery Grizzard Trail. The Sewanee Natural Bridge offers a breathtaking view of three states. There are also 150 miles of hiking trails as well as a range of recreational activities available for visitors.

South Cumberland State Recreation Area, 11745 US 41, Monteagle, TN 37356 (931-924-2980; www.tn.gov/environment /parks/SouthCumberland)

⌒ Arlington

> *The coach rolled through the small iron gates, up the slight rise, toward massive white columns. Lee had not see Arlington for nearly three years, saw again the pure size, the exaggerated grandeur. It was the home of George Washington Parke Custis, the grandson of Martha Washington and Lee's father-in-law, and the old man had built the mansion more as a showplace for the artifacts of President Washington than as a home for a living family. The design was cold, impractical, but to Custis, the impression was the important thing, the shrine to his revered ancestors. But now Custis was dead.*
>
> —JEFF SHAARA, *Gods and Generals*

AS YOU APPROACH Arlington National Cemetery from Washington and drive over Memorial Bridge, the white-columned Custis-Lee Mansion stands like a sentinel in the distance overlooking the city and the Potomac River.

From the visitors center, you can easily walk to the **McClellan Gate** and find lines from Kentucky writer Theodore O'Hara's poem "Bivouac of the Dead." Written to honor the Kentucky troops who were killed in 1847 during the Mexican-American War, O'Hara's memorable lines are inscribed on the gate: "On Fame's eternal camping-ground, their silent tents are spread, and Glory guards, with solemn round, the bivouac of the dead."

Arlington National Cemetery is the final resting place for many distinguished individuals, presidents, and military leaders. A tour through this somber place begins at the visitors center, where exhibits, a bookstore, and photographs detail its history and legacy in American history. The Tomb of the Unknown Soldier is found here, along with the grave sites of President John F. Kennedy, Jacqueline Kennedy, Ted Kennedy, and Robert Kennedy. Walking the cemetery's hills and byways affords an unmatched glimpse into American history.

⑨ LITERARY LODGING

THE WILLARD INTERCONTINENTAL HOTEL

Few hotels in Washington can match the pedigreed history of the Willard. Two blocks from the White House, the hotel was boarded

$\mathcal{V}$IRGINIA

$\mathbf{V}$ IRGINIA'S NATURAL GEOGRAPHIC BEAUTY is among the
South's most diverse. From the Blue Ridge and Allegheny
Mountains to shimmering coastal areas and the Chincoteague
barrier island—Virginia reveals a host of sites and surprises.

The state is also a living history book. Almost everywhere you turn
in the Old Dominion, a page or chapter in American history can be discovered and relived. At the battlefields of Yorktown, Manassas, Bull Run,
and Fredericksburg, you will be met with compelling American stories.

This bountiful land that was the richest of the 13 original colonies
has inspired noted writers: Douglas Southall Freeman, who received a
Pulitzer Prize for his comprehensive biography of Robert E. Lee; contemporary author William Styron, who fondly recalled his Virginia boy
hood in *Lie Down in Darkness;* Edgar Allan Poe, whose affection f
Richmond and Virginia never wavered. Tom Wolfe (*The Right Stuff*) a
Ellen Glasgow (*In This Our Life*) both had significant Richmond ties. Sl
wood Anderson and William Faulkner settled in the state in their
years, while Willa Cather was born in Frederick County.

Yet no name on the list of Virginia's literary lights can top that
most profound writer, Thomas Jefferson, our third president. Jeff
innate love of the land and of his home at Monticello shaped th
ration of Independence.

A literary journey through Virginia promises to be unforge

up during the 1960s and would have fallen to the wrecking ball had it not been for Oliver Carr Company, which miraculously saved the stately structure that is one of the city's most beloved landmarks. Restored to its former glory, the Willard reopened on August 20, 1986, after nearly 20 years of neglect.

The list of celebrated authors who have strolled the Willard's corridors is long. The striking Beaux-Arts architecture is credited to Henry Janeway Hardenbergh, who also designed New York's Plaza Hotel and the Waldorf-Astoria. Since 1853 the hotel has hosted every US president from Franklin Pierce to George W. Bush.

Author Nathaniel Hawthorne stayed here while covering the Civil War for *The Atlantic Monthly* and wrote, "This hotel, in fact, may be more justly called the center of Washington and the Union than either the Capitol, the White House, or the State Department. . . . you exchange nods with governors of sovereign states; you elbow illustrious men, and tread on the toes of generals; you hear statesmen and orators speaking in their familiar tones. You are mixed up with office seekers, wire pullers, inventors, artists, poets, posers . . . until identity is lost among them."

Throughout its history journalist and writers have enjoyed the **Round Robin Bar,** whose walls are outlined with images of the literary greats who have graced its halls. Mark Twain, Charles Dickens, and Walt Whitman delighted in the Willard's amenities and proximity to both White House and halls of Congress. Suites are named after Presidents Abraham Lincoln, John Adams, Thomas Jefferson, and George Washington.

Willard InterContinental Hotel, 1401 Pennsylvania Avenue NW , Washington, DC 20004 (1-866-487-2537; http://washington.intercontinental.com)

❀ EXCURSIONS AND DIVERSIONS

ARLINGTON HOUSE

The nation's capital abounds with museums and monuments, many free of charge and open year-round. If you make the trek to Arlington, however, be sure to inspect **Arlington House,** also known as the **Custis-Lee Mansion.** This structure affords one of the grandest views available of the Federal City. Robert E. Lee lived here until the Civil War began, when it was designated as part of Arlington National Cemetery. The plantation estate has many artifacts that belonged to the Lee family with many reproductions of that period. All three of Lee's sons who survived the Civil War shared one room in the house. A tour through the house, gardens, and slave quarters is recommended following your Arlington National Cemetery tour. The house today serves as a memorial to Lee.

Arlington House, 321 Sherman Drive, Fort Myer, VA 22211 (703-235-1530; www.nps.gov/arho)

ᴄᴧ Charlottesville

They have nearly finished the Rotunda—The pillars of the Portico are completed and it greatly improves the appearance of the whole—The books are removed into the library—and we have a very fine collection.
—EDGAR ALLAN POE, LETTER TO JOHN ALLAN, 1826

ON CAMPUS AT THE UNIVERSITY OF VIRGINIA

THE LUSHLY LANDSCAPED CAMPUS of "Mr. Jefferson's academical village"—the University of Virginia—lies at the heart of Charlottesville. A university town in the truest sense, the hilly enclave in the center of Albemarle County is reminiscent of "Old Virginia" at its best. Rambling horse farms, wineries, manor houses, and a pastoral landscape accent the academic atmosphere.

The memory of Thomas Jefferson haunts every corner of the village, from Michie Tavern, to the Lawn at the University of Virginia, to Monticello, Jefferson's proudest architectural achievement. Edgar Allan Poe is the most renowned literary name associated with the university, while Jefferson is the most revered. William Faulkner's name is also on its literary roster.

Poe arrived from Richmond to begin his college studies on February 14, 1826. He occupied a small room just off the Lawn at **13 West Range,** today marked by a plaque just outside the site. The Spartan room—

maintained by the Raven Society—is where Poe spent many nights reading, writing, and entertaining fellow students with his enthralling stories. You can listen to a short tape about his life at the university while peering into the room through the Plexiglas window. A wooden sculpture of a black raven stands guard on the windowsill as a vivid reminder of its most famous former tenant.

When Poe arrived at the university, Jefferson was still designing his grand plan for it. Many of the buildings were still under construction. Poe was the 136th student out of the 177 registered for the second semester. His studies included modern and ancient languages under Professors Long and Batterman. He achieved top honors in French and Latin and was elected to the Literary and Debating Society.

The **Rotunda** overlooks the Lawn and remains the university's most recognizable landmark designed by Jefferson. Inside you'll discover a small etched pane of glass from the 13 West Range room on which Poe reputedly wrote a stanza from one of his poems: "O Thou timid one, do not let thy / Form slumber within these / Unhallowed walls, / For herein lies

/ The ghost of an awful crime." During the school year tours of the university led by students depart from the Rotunda.

Within walking distance from here is the **Alderman Library.** A bust of Poe is found in the library's main reading room.

As a student Poe worked on "Tamerlane" and later "A Tale of the Ragged Mountains." While in residence, he is believed to have visited Mr. Jefferson at Monticello, who frequently invited students from the university to tea or dinner. There

BUST OF POE AT THE ALDERMAN LIBRARY

is also a story that Poe attended Jefferson's funeral. None of these events can be confirmed—but they could have happened, since Jefferson knew many of the friends of John Allan, Poe's foster father.

POE'S BLACK RAVEN, A SCULPTURE
IN HIS ROOM AT UVA

Like most of Poe's stories, his life at the university did not have a happy ending: He was asked to leave on December 15, 1826, due to gambling debts of $2,000 that he had accrued playing cards. John Allan refused to pay the debts, leaving the writer little choice but to abandon his studies. The university was insistent that unless he paid off his debts he could not continue his studies.

Poe reluctantly left Charlottesville for Richmond. There he struggled to earn a living as a writer along with engaging in numerous confrontations with Allan. Eventually he would travel to West Point and enroll in the military school, but he soon found that military life was not to his liking. His vagabond life continued, taking him to South Carolina, New York, and eventually Baltimore, where he died in 1849. Had he been able to complete his studies at the University of Virginia, his life most likely would have taken a different turn.

The Poe sites are all open to the public.

William Faulkner in Charlottesville

The Mississippi writer who created his own literary universe with Yoknapatawpha County came to Charlottesville in 1957 as the University of Virginia's first writer in residence. With his reputation as one of America's most preeminent authors firmly established, Faulkner accepted the prestigious post for two reasons: He considered the university one of the nation's finest, and his daughter Jill Faulkner Summers lived nearby with her family in Albemarle County.

Faulkner first visited the area in 1931 to attend the Southern Writers Conference. When he accepted the writer-in-residence post, which had an annual salary of $2,000, he remarked, "Don't worry about the money, don't pay me anything—it would only confuse my tax situation and besides I don't know whether I'll be any good at this or not. All I need is enough money to buy a little whiskey and tobacco. Let me work at it awhile and see how it goes." Rather than structured classes, the Nobel Prize winner held informal sessions answering questions about his work and American literature in general with his pipe nearby.

The author responsible for 16 novels relished his time in the Virginia hamlet, frequently mingling frequently with students and townspeople. An affable and likable southern gentleman, Faulkner took long walks along Rugby Road on his way to classes wearing his familiar tweed jacket and tie. An avid horseman, on many afternoons he could be spotted at sporting events or riding horses. His classes were usually overflowing with students or locals who managed to sneak in to hear him. His classes were overflowing with students and the locals who managed to sneak in.

Faulkner often reminisced about his experiences in Charlottesville, once writing that he was "just a writer-in-residence, not the speaker-in-residence." It was here that he penned much of *The Mansion* and several other noted works. His fondest wish in his later years was to make Charlottesville his permanent home. Not only did he want to be near his grandsons, but he had grown fond of the Virginia landscape and its people, who respected his privacy. Unlike Oxford, Mississippi—where Faulkner grew up, and everyone knew where he lived—the Virginia countryside allowed him a quiet life.

He found the ideal retirement spot at Red Acres, a 250-acre farm 9 miles from Charlottesville overlooking the Blue Ridge Mountains with a stable and smokehouse. But Faulkner's dream would not be realized. Heading back to Rowan Oak in 1962 to settle family matters, he was thrown by a horse and suffered a debilitating fall. Within days the pain became excruciating. He was taken to White Sanitarium in Byhalia, where he quietly passed from a heart attack on July 6.

Faulkner's goal at the university was simple: He wanted to help "create an atmosphere," and indeed he did. His legacy continues today at the **Alderman Library Special Collections of Albert and Shirley Small,** which holds the distinction of housing one of the largest collections of Faulkner's manuscripts anywhere. Most of the classroom sessions that were recorded have been digitized; photographs and letters are also available for viewing. But somehow Faulkner's presence is best felt as you walk along Rugby Road or gaze up at the Rotunda. It's comforting to know that the years he spent here were most likely the most serene and peaceful of his career.

Alderman Library Special Collections of Albert & Shirley Small (434-243-1776; http://small.library.virginia.edu)

Monticello

The natural beauty in and around Charlottesville adds to your Poe, Faulkner, and Jefferson outings. Once you have peeked inside Poe's room and examined William Faulkner's collection or listened to his tapes, head up to Jefferson's Monticello or "little mountain," which affords an exceptional overview of Albemarle County and Virginia's lush countryside in addition to one of the most revered presidential estates in the country.

A tour through Mr. Jefferson's Monticello retreat is easily a two- to three-hour commitment, depending on how much you want to see at the house and the **Thomas Jefferson Visitors Center.** The author of the Declaration of Independence, one of the most important documents drafted by our founding fathers, was a native son of Virginia.

The third president of the United States spent 33 years in public life, serving also as governor of Virginia, secretary of state, and minister to France. Jefferson designed every aspect of Monticello, with most furnishings of the three-story, 21-room house revealing aspects of his tastes and personality. His remarkable genius and creativity as an architect, writer, statesman, inventor, and president are on display at this presidential home.

Jefferson called Monticello his "essay in architecture," and he completed it in 1768. Many of his personal items and treasures can be found inside the graceful mansion, including books, china, and furniture; you can also see ingenious designs like the dumbwaiter in the dining room. He borrowed heavily from Italian architect Andrea Palladio and spent 40 years designing and redesigning every aspect of the house. A dome, the first used in an American home, was his idea for bringing outside light into the house and at the same time adding to the exterior appearance. His love of France is also clearly exhibited. Most of the furnishings and draperies are designs he chose while serving as secretary of state.

The visitors center is where your Monticello experience begins. Here you'll find a brief film on Jefferson's life, exhibits, a café, and a gift shop. This is also where you catch the van to head up to Monticello, with a bronze statue of Mr. Jefferson leading the way.

A tour of Monticello encompasses the parlor, the hall, bedroom, dining room, and book room. The gardens with their panoramic views complete your visit. Peer through an opening in the trees and you will see the Rotunda at the University of Virginia. This spot is especially lovely in springtime, when the azaleas and camellias are in full bloom. Mulberry Row holds the cook's room, stables, and outbuildings that were integral to the operation of Monticello. Jefferson is buried on the property, along with other members of his family. His epitaph reads, "Author of the Declaration of American Independence, of the Statute of Virginia for Religious Freedom, and Father of the University of Virginia."

Special and after-hour tours can be arranged through the visitors center. During the holiday season, Monticello is bedecked in colonial Christmas splendor.

Thomas Jefferson Visitor Center and Smith Education Center, 931 Thomas Jefferson Parkway, Charlottesville, VA 22902 (434-984-9800; www.monticello.org)

🍂 LITERARY LODGING

KESWICK HALL

Keswick remains Charlottesville's most historic lodging. Located just 6 miles east of Charlottesville and 5 miles from Monticello, Keswick Hall is a genuine travel-back-in-time experience. With its country-manor ambience, formal tea, and ornate Italianate architecture—and set on over 600 acres of Virginia's countryside—this property is a favorite lodging choice while visiting Charlottesville.

Built as a private residence in 1912 and named Villa Crawford, it has undergone a series of owners and incarnations. Formerly owned by Sir Bernard Ashley, husband of designer Laura Ashley, today the 48-room hotel is owned and managed by the same group as Richmond's Jefferson Hotel. The Tuscan-style villa on the edge of the Blue Ridge has been a favorite for both the Hollywood and the literary set. It has an 18-hole golf course, spa, indoor/outdoor pool, tennis courts, and fitness center. A Virginia library includes more than 400 volumes about the state or works written by Virginia authors—including John Grisham and Rita Mae Brown, who have homes nearby. With afternoon tea served daily, Keswick closely resembles a country estate with a British accent. You can also arrange to go horseback riding through the Virginia countryside or fly fishing at any number of streams found near Charlottesville. Visiting this property is an experience and destination in itself.

Keswick Hall, 701 Club Drive, Keswick, VA 22947 (434-979-3440; www.keswick.com)

✿ EXCURSIONS AND DIVERSIONS

A RELISH FOR WINE

Thomas Jefferson's love of wine ("in nothing have the habits of the palate more decisive influence than in our relish of wines," he wrote) has spilled out into his neighborhood. Charlottesville has become the wine center of Virginia, not surprising with more than 20 wineries throughout the region. Over half of Virginia's 2,000 vineyard acres are found in the area, and the state is the fifth largest producer of wine in the United States. The **Monticello Wine Trail** is not to be missed. Featured along the route are wineries small and large, including Barboursville Vineyards, Keswick Vineyards, Horton Vineyards, Jefferson Vineyards, and Stone Mountain Vineyards, to name just a few. The **Monticello Wine Festival** is usually held during the spring; events on the estate grounds range from wine tours to tastings, live music, exhibits, entertainment, and more.

Michie Tavern is situated roughly a mile from Monticello, so before you explore Jefferson's home, enjoy a delicious southern-style lunch of fried chicken, mashed potatoes, corn bread, and green beans at this historic tavern. The original building dates back to 1784 and is only open for lunch. It is a great way to prepare for your tour of Monticello or the University of Virginia!

Another annual event that attracts writers and literary fans from around the country is the **Virginia Festival of the Book**—a five-day event held in early spring.

Monticello Wine Trail (www.monticellowinetrail.com)

Monticello Wine Festival (www.monticello.org)

Mitchie Tavern, 683 Thomas Jefferson Parkway, Charlottesville, VA 22902 (434-977-1234; www.michietavern.com)

Virginia Festival of the Book (www.vabook.org)

Charlottesville CVB, PO Box 178, Charlottesville, VA (1-877-386-1103, www.visitcharlottesville.org)

ᥲ Chincoteague

Tom's point was a protected piece of land where the marsh was hard
and the grass especially sweet. About seventy wild ponies, exhausted by
their morning's run, stood browsing quietly, as if they were in a corral.
Only occasionally they looked up at their captors.

—MARGUERITE HENRY, *Misty of Chincoteague*

VIRGINIA'S BARRIER ISLAND Chincoteague is endowed with a serene
landscape that was captured in Marguerite Henry's children's classic *Misty
of Chincoteague*. Windswept beaches, fishing, crabbing, and legends of pirates
and shipwrecks off the coastline add to the intrigue. But the site is best
known for its famed Pony Penning Days, which take place every summer
and continue to draw travelers. Chincoteague's resident wild ponies are
believed to descendants of horses that escaped from Spanish galleons.

Visiting Chincoteague, roughly a four-hour drive from Washington,
DC, offers an opportunity to traipse through literary history and view the
landscape that became the background for the popular children's book.
The area is also blessed with two outstanding nature refuges—the Chincoteague National Refuge and the Assateague National Seashore.

Henry's writing career began as a child when her father, who was a
publisher, gave her a desk as a Christmas present. Growing up, books became her favorite pastime with Zane Grey among her favorite authors.
Henry would go on to write 59 books, most dealing with horses.

In the midst of her career, Henry's editor persuaded her to visit the
island and write about its elusive wild ponies. Chincoteague residents Paul
and Maureen Beebe became the models for two of her novel's characters,
whose most fervent wish was to own a wild pony. The book was published
in 1947 and became an immediate success; it was turned into a movie in
1961.

One of Henry's last trips to the island was in 1960, when she visited
the Beebes and spent several weeks reminiscing about her ongoing affection
for Chincoteague and how *Misty* had changed her life. In addition to Miss
Molly's Inn (see "Literary Lodging"), there is a statue of Misty near the
town square. The **Chincoteague Pony Centre** is entirely devoted to the
movie and book. Vintage photographs, Marguerite Henry's books, artwork
by the books illustrator Wesley Dennis, and original *Misty* movie posters

are found in this museum. There is also a 30-minute documentary on the island and the wild ponies.

Chincoteague Pony Centre, 6417 Carriage Drive, Chincoteague Island, VA 23336 (757-336-2776; www.chincoteague.com/pony centre)

⚜ LITERARY LODGING

THE MARGUERITE HENRY CONNECTION

Miss Molly's Inn, built in 1894, was a favorite haunt of author Marguerite Henry and is where she stayed for two weeks in 1946 to write *Misty of Chincoteague.* The front porch was her favorite spot to work. Henry credited the inn for allowing her the peace and privacy she needed to pen her book. Today the seven-bedroom Victorian inn features the Marguerite Henry Room, where the author resided; it is one of the inn's most requested rooms. Lace curtains and a fireplace create a relaxing ambience. Miss Molly's serves a gourmet breakfast, an English tea, and refreshments in the gazebo. It's conveniently located near everything in the town. Boogie boards and beach cruisers are also available for guests.

Channel Bass Inn is where Henry stayed following the book's publication. You'll get a genuine taste of England at this cozy seven-room hostelry where English tea is served several days a week. Guests have access to complimentary bikes, bird books, beach towels, and coolers during their visit.

The Refuge Inn has to be on the loveliest on the island and is another excellent choice. Larger than Miss Molly's or Channel Bass, the Refuge Inn is a luxurious facility in an elegant woodland setting. Complimentary breakfast, an indoor/outdoor pool, and bike rentals for guests are offered. The Baywatch Cottage is a very special accommodation. Reminiscent of Cape Cod, this cottage is rented by the week during the high season and available for mini-week rentals in the off-season. Staying here is an exceptional experience for those seeing solace and serenity in an unspoiled setting. Often the Chincoteague ponies can be seen grazing outside the windows as well as an array of birds, including ospreys and shorebirds. White-tailed deer also inhabit this area of the island.

Miss Molly's Inn, 4141 Main Street, Chincoteague, VA 23336 (1-800-221-5620; http://missmollys-inn.com)

Channel Bass Inn, 6228 Church Street, Chincoteague, VA 23336 (757-336-6148; http://channelbassinn.com)

The Refuge Inn, 7058 Maddox Boulevard, Chincoteague, VA 23336 (1-888-257-0038; www.refugeinn.com)

⊛ EXCURSIONS AND DIVERSIONS

CHINCOTEAGUE NATIONAL WILDLIFE REFUGE

Beautiful unspoiled landscapes abound in this corner of Virginia. Sailing, birding, hiking, kayaking, and miles upon miles of watery inlets and islands are found at the **Chincoteague National Wildlife Refuge,** which incorporates some of Virginia's most pristine landscapes. Wild marshes and never-ending vistas of untouched vegetation comprise the 14,000 acres of seashore forest. The refuge's prime location along the Atlantic Flyway makes it a birding hot spot.

Established in 1943 to provide a habitat for migratory birds, the scenic seashore is also a popular haven for cyclists, surf fishermen, swimmers, and horseback riders. The Herbert H. Bateman Educational and Administrative Center is an ideal starting point for your outdoor outing. The center houses exhibits about the island's nature trails and wildlife habitats. It also provides information about the various trails within the refuge.

A bevy of bird life and other fauna can be discovered in this pristine terrain. White-tailed deer call the refuge home, along with the wild Chincoteague ponies. Feral descendants of colonial horses transported to Assateague in the 17th century, these are the ponies that so inspired author Marguerite Henry in *Misty of Chincoteague.* They can be seen from several locations. A fence along the Virginia/Maryland state line separates the island's ponies into two herds. The Maryland herd is owned by the National Park Service whereas the Virginia herd is owned by the Chincoteague Fire Company, which stages the annual **Pony Penning Days** on the last Wednesday and Thursday in July.

The refuge is also home to red foxes, river otters, and muskrats. Among the birds that can be spotted are marbled godwits, mallards, black scoters, piping plovers, snow geese, egrets, glossy ibises, red-tailed hawks, and ospreys. The **Wildlife Loop** is among the prettiest trails here—a 3.25-mile loop encircling freshwater impoundments ideal for observing wading birds. Another popular trail is the **Woodland Trail,** which meanders through a lush pine forest and leads to an overlook where visitors can often spot the wild ponies. The **Lighthouse Trail** is a 0.25-mile foot path that eventually ends at the Assateague Lighthouse.

Venturing back into town along Main Street, you will discover a range of unique shops, art galleries, and ice cream parlors, making your visit to Chincoteague a truly Americana experience.

Chincoteague National Wildlife Refuge, 8231 Beach Road, Chincoteague Island, VA 23336 (757-336-6122; www.fws.gov /northeast/chinco)

Pony Penning Days (www.chincoteague.com/ponies.html)

ᏛᎳ Lynchburg

THE MAIN SUPPLY BASE for the Confederate army during the Civil War and namesake of John Lynch, Lynchburg, one hour south of Charlottesville, has two major literary associations. On the National Register of Historic Places, "the City of Seven Hills" boasts of Douglas Southall Freeman, eminent biographer of Virginians George Washington and Robert E. Lee. He was awarded the Pulitzer Prize for both. Anne Spencer, the noted African American poet affiliated with the Harlem Renaissance, also lived in town.

Freeman, who was born in Lynchburg but spent most of his formative years in Richmond, began his journalism career at the *Richmond Times Dispatch* and became editor of the *Richmond News Leader*. After publishing *Lee's Dispatches,* he was approached by Charles Scribner & Sons to write a biography of Lee. This book involved exhaustive and meticulous research. It was published in 1934 and 1935 and awarded the Pulitzer Prize; it remains the definitive biography of the Confederate general. Freeman's former family home is located at **416 Main Street,** where a Virginia Historical Marker pays tribute to the Virginia author.

Spencer, who moved to the city in 1893, was recognized by James Weldon, who published her work in *The Book of American Negro Poetry*. She is the second African American poet to be included in *The Norton Anthology of Modern Poetry*. The home where Spencer resided from 1903 until 1925 is found at **1313 Pierce Street**. Her literary friends and visitors included Langston Hughes and Alex Haley.

Spencer's poetry was written on anything available, including the walls of her Pierce Street home. The two-story Queen Anne has been restored and displays many of her personal belongings. Photographs, writings, and memorabilia are on view. The garden area is where she spent much of her time and is the real charm of a visit.

The Anne Spencer House & Garden Museum, 1313 Pierce Street, Lynchburg, VA 24501 (434-845-1313; www.anne spencermuseum.com)

ᕗ Newport News

> *Riding down to Port Warwick from Richmond, the train begins to pick up speed on the outskirts of the city, past the tobacco factories with their ever-present haze of acrid, sweetish dust and past rows of uniformity brown clapboard houses which stretch down the hilly streets for miles, it seems, the hundreds of rooftops all reflecting the pale light of dawn. . . . Suddenly the train burrowing through the pinewoods, and the conductor, who looks middle-aged and respectable like someone's favorite uncle, lurches through the car asking for tickets. . . . Port Warwick is a ship-building city and the workers' houses begin where the marshlands end—the clean cheap clusters of plywood cottages.*
>
> —WILLIAM STYRON, *Lie Down in Darkness*

IT WAS IN THIS ONCE THRIVING and prosperous shipbuilding port that novelist William Styron, author of *Sophie's Choice* and *The Confessions of Nat Turner*, spent his childhood in an area called Hilton Village. Educated at Christ Church School, Davidson College, and Duke University, Styron tapped into his Virginia boyhood and memories from his southern up-bringing to write *A Tidewater Morning: Three Tales from Youth* and *Lie Down in Darkness*.

But although he enjoyed the stability of a middle-class upbringing, his early years were also marked with sadness: His mother passed away from cancer when he was a young teen, and he was mostly raised by his father. Their time together was precious to him as an only child, but the passing of his mother made an indelible and memorable impression on both his philosophy and his life. Although he spent the majority of his adult life in New York and New England, he never forgot his Virginia heritage.

"I wanted to be a writer and nothing else . . . and I realized this is what I have to do with my life." Although Styron worked in New York publishing, he was determined to tell compelling stories. *Lie Down in Darkness* was his first novel, published in 1951. Styron won the Pulitzer Prize in 1967 for *The Confessions of Nat Turner.* At times the controversial novel threw him into a whirlwind of publicity.

Although the house Styron grew up has been destroyed, the city of Newport News decided to honor its most famous literary son by building **Port Warwick** in 2001, a 3-acre mixed-use community where his name and literary accomplishments are honored in a plaque in the center of the village. Styron was actively involved both with the planning and the design of the project that bears his name. Two main boulevards leading to Port Warwick are named Loftis Boulevard and Nat Turner Boulevard—both characters from his novels. The remaining streets in the attractive community honor other writers, with the names selected by Styron himself.

"I have chosen," he said, "outstanding American literary figures from the nineteenth and twentieth century. These artists seem to me ones who are indisputably lodged in the pantheon of American literature. Limitation in number has forced me to exclude many illustrious writers deserving of recognition, therefore my choices reflect a personal leaning. But the overall selection of names does, I think, represent the best in the great flowering of American literary art." F. Scott Fitzgerald, Thomas Wolfe, John Steinbeck, Emily Dickinson, Herman Melville, and Mark Twain's names are all visible as you walk around the community.

Styron attended Port Warwick's dedication ceremony in 2001 and selected quotations that appear on the marble base of a Masaru Bando sculpture on Philip Roth Street. A plaque in the center of the community details Styron's literary accomplishments. The Newport News Library also remembers him and has an extensive collection of his novels. The Port Warwick Conservancy and Foundation offer a series of cultural events throughout the year.

Port Warwick (www.portwarwick.com; www.theportwarwick conservancy.com)

🐚 LITERARY LODGING

THE WILLIAMSBURG INN

Millionaire John D. Rockefeller's dream of creating a world-class hotel in one of Virginia's loveliest settings became a reality when the Williamsburg Inn, opened for business in 1937. Envisioning a "home away from home," Rockefeller became involved with every detail in the inn's intricate planning, from the lush landscaping to the décor and furnishings. The ambience of the white-columned beauty reflects the taste of the 18th century coupled with all the amenities of the 21st. Guest rooms are designed in three styles: floral, classic, and restoration. Large marble showers and Thiebault bed linens accentuate the antique furnishings and silk window treatments.

The inn recaptures the ambience of a Virginia country estate in the Old South with pronounced English touches throughout. The inn has hosted an impressive array of notables throughout its history, including Queen Elizabeth II and Prince Philip, Sir Winston Churchill, former President Dwight Eisenhower, President Ronald Reagan, and former Prime Minister of Great Britain Margaret Thatcher.

The dining areas are every bit as appealing as the guest rooms. The Regency Room borrows elements from the Royal Pavilion in Brighton, England, including hand-painted Oriental panels, crystal chandeliers, and palm-leafed columns. Birders, bikers, hikers, and golfers will all find plenty to do in this pastoral Virginia setting.

Williamsburg Inn, 136 East Francis Street, Williamsburg, VA 23185 (1-800-447-8679; www.colonialwilliamsburg.com/stay /williamsburg-inn)

⚜ EXCURSIONS AND DIVERSIONS

DISCOVERING MARITIME HISTORY

The Mariners' Museum near Port Warwick makes an ideal spot for discovering Virginia's maritime heritage. One of the finest nautical museums in the country, it exhibits a treasure trove of nautical artifacts—more than 35,000—including the anchor from the Civil War ironclad *Monitor*, John Smith's map of the Chesapeake Bay, and the polar bear figurehead from Admiral Richard Byrd's 1950s Antarctica expedition.

August Crabtree's miniature ship collection is perhaps the museum's most prized holding, along with the marine paintings of Fitzhugh Lane and William Trost. Its galleries also offer an in-depth look at the US Navy and the important role it has played in the nation's history. The accomplishments of Admiral Horatio Alger, John Paul Jones, and David Farragut are featured on the self-guided tour. You'll find a detailed history of the Chesapeake Bay as well. The gleaming white contemporary facility is highly recommended for anyone with an interest in the sea and ships.

The building is located within **Mariners' Museum Park,** a 550-acre woodland ideal for hiking and picnics that overlooks Lake Maury. The 5-mile Noland Trail given to the museum in 1991 by the Noland family has 14 bridges, including the Lions Bridge, which was donated in 1932 by museum founder Archer Milton Huntington.

The Mariners' Museum, 100 Museum Drive, Newport News, VA 23606 (1-800-581-7245; www.marinersmuseum.org)

⌒ Richmond

> *I am a Virginian—at least I call myself one, for I have resided all my life . . . in Richmond.*
>
> —EDGAR ALLAN POE

WITH HIS BLACK CAPE FLOWING in the chilly night, and having left his walking stick behind at the Swan Tavern where he was living, Poe fled Richmond in the dark of night following a visit to Elmira Shelton, his first love. It was September 1849. He boarded a boat at Rockett's Landing heading to Baltimore, where he would catch a train to Philadelphia and New York. His plan was to eventually return to Richmond, but two weeks following his departure he mysteriously passed away in Baltimore, adding to the Poe mystery.

A trip to Richmond provides insight into Poe's troubled and tumultuous life. The poet who created such eloquently haunting poems as "The Raven," and "Annabel Lee" died on October 7, 1849, but his story is one of the most dramatic in literary history, and Richmond is by far the most intriguing stop along the Poe trail. Although his restless demeanor took him everywhere from Boston, his birthplace, to Baltimore, where he is buried, he considered himself a Virginian.

Orphaned at age three following his mother's death and father's desertion, Poe was raised by John and Frances Allan. His life was marked by constant financial struggle and an ongoing difficult relationship with his foster father. Richmond played a significant part in Poe's life as well; it is where he grew up, began his writing career at the *Southern Literary Messenger,* and fell in love with Elmira Royster before leaving for the University of Virginia. Though he lived here only off and on through his later years, he considered Richmond home and planned to return to the city of his youth in the final days of his life. And indeed it was one of the last places he visited prior to his death in Baltimore, making it a must for Poe fans.

Poe landmarks are everywhere in Virginia's capital city, where the rock-strewn James River flows freely throughout the downtown area. These sites are easily accessible by either walking or driving from the **Edgar Allan Poe Museum** at 1914 East Main Street. This facility houses one of the largest and most comprehensive collections of Poe artifacts and memorabilia in the country, if not the world. Located in the Old Stone House—one of Richmond's oldest buildings, dating back to Poe's era—the facility concentrates more on Poe's enormous literary gifts than on the myths that have arisen over the years about his tormented life. The museum consists of four buildings joined together with a courtyard in the center.

Poe was born into a family of actors on January 19, 1809. He was left in the care of his foster parents following his mother's death from tuberculosis. Frances Allan cared for Elizabeth Poe when she was ill, and following her death the young Edgar was taken in by the family but never officially adopted. His brother William was left with the Clemm family

STONE BUST OF POE

in Baltimore, while his sister Rosalie was adopted by the McKenzie family in Richmond. Although the Allans were a prominent Richmond family, John Allan, a wealthy tobacco merchant, was not a warm father figure. Poe never enjoyed a loving family environment. As he grew older in particular, he and his foster father were constantly at odds about Poe's decision to become a writer.

The museum tells the story behind his tormented but brilliant literary life through family heirlooms and mementos, artifacts, letters, and memorabilia. Some of the museum's most prized possessions include the Poe family Bible, Poe's walking stick, his boyhood bed, Virginia Clemm Poe's trinket box, the poet's vest, and a lock of his hair.

The story behind the walking stick is of particular interest. On Poe's last visit to Richmond, just two weeks before his death in Baltimore, he left this stick behind. The story goes that Poe visited his family physician, Dr. John Carter, on his last evening in Richmond and picked up Carter's sword cane inadvertently. After Poe's death, Carter retrieved his cane from Poe's room at the Swan Tavern, but he kept Poe's walking stick instead of returning it to the author's relatives. When the museum opened in 1922, it bought the stick for $250; if you look closely you can see "Poe" engraved on the silver tip.

Poe's personal trunk is on view, as is a daguerreotype of Poe, his autobiography, and *Poems of 1831*, along with personal letters and furniture from the Allans. Plan to devote at least two hours here perusing these prized possessions, which provide excellent insight into his life and literary career.

Perhaps the loveliest section of the museum is the Enchanted Garden, where a stone bust of Poe, donated in 1931, is the centerpiece of the loggia. The loggia is constructed with bricks from the *Southern Literary Messenger,* the magazine responsible for launching Poe's literary career and where he worked as an editor at age 26.

Another key Poe site is located at 2407 West Grace Street: **the home of Elmira Royster Shelton**—the poet's first and greatest love—where she lived during his last visit to the city. The house is privately owned and can only be viewed from the outside, but its significance is paramount since it is one of the last addresses Poe visited before departing for Baltimore.

Poe, an admirer of Lord Byron, was a romantic at heart and fell in love with Royster when he was just 16 and she, 15. They were neighbors growing up; before he left to study at the University of Virginia in 1826 he secretly proposed to her, professing that he would one day return to Richmond and marry her. While at the university Poe wrote her daily missives expressing his affection. However, her father, who disapproved of the relationship, destroyed all his letters. Feeling abandoned and forgotten, she married Alexander Shelton, an event that would haunt Poe throughout his life. Brokenhearted, he carried the memory of his first and lost love with him. Poe scholars believe that "Tamerlane" and other poems he wrote as a youth were inspired by his failed romance with Royster.

Poe and Royster's paths crossed again in 1848, when Poe was in Richmond on a lecture tour. Royster, now a widow, attended, sitting in the front row and rekindling their romance. In a letter she recalled his visit to her house and wrote, "I was ready to go to church and a servant told me that a gentleman in the parlor wanted to see me. I went down and was amazed to see him—but knew him instantly."

Poe recounted his love for her in a letter to Maria Clemm: "I think she loves me more devotedly than anyone I ever knew . . . I cannot help loving her in return." He once again asked for her hand in marriage, and visited her and his physician, Dr. John Carter, before he left Richmond on the evening of September 27, 1849. Carter strongly advised him against taking such a long journey with his failing health.

In her later years Royster remembered Poe's final visit and wrote, "He came up to my house on the evening of the 26th Sept. to take leave of me. He was very sad, and complained of being quite sick. I felt his pulse, and found he had considerable fever, and did not think it probable he would be able to start the next morning (Thursday) as he anticipated. I felt so wretched about him all that night, that I went up early the next morning to inquire after him, when, much to my regret, he had left in the boat for Baltimore."

In his haste to leave Richmond, and perhaps because Shelton had not made a firm commitment to marry him, he left his trunk behind, confirming that he had planned to return to Richmond following his lecture tours in Philadelphia and New York.

But his arrival in Baltimore is shrouded in mystery and controversy. While in the city he became very ill, many think due to heavy rains, drinking heavily, and not taking care of himself. On October 3, a young printer found Poe lying unconscious outside Gunner's Hall and rushed him to the Washington College Hospital, where he died on October 7, 1849. The debate goes on today as to the exact cause of Poe's demise. One thing is certain: He planned to return to Richmond, marry Elmira Shelton, and begin his literary career anew.

The Elmira Royster Shelton home is a private residence and is just behind **St. John's Church,** 2319 East Broad Street, where Poe's mother is interred along with T. W. White, former editor of the *Southern Literary Messenger.* St. John's is one of Richmond most historic churches—this is where Patrick Henry delivered his "Give me Liberty or give me Death" speech.

The **Virginia State Capitol**—a healthy stroll or drive away from the museum at 1000 Bank Street—holds a life-sized bronze sculpture of the writer. On many days a red-tailed hawk stands guard near the piece, which was a 1958 gift. Poe is seated with a book and pen in his hands.

The final stop on your Richmond Poe tour should be the **Monumental Church,** 1224 East Broad Street, another of Richmond's most important architectural landmarks. The church, designed by Robert Mills, Thomas Jefferson's only protégé, was constructed as a memorial to the victims of a devastating fire that destroyed the Richmond Theatre in December 1811. Listed on the National Register of Historic Places and near Capital Square, this is where Poe worshipped as a child with the Allans, who occupied Pew 80. The church is managed by the Historic Richmond Foundation and is open only by appointment.

POE SCULPTURE AT THE VIRGINIA STATE CAPITOL

The Library of Virginia, 800 East Broad Street, is also recommended, as it houses many of Poe's letters and personal artifacts.

Edgar Allan Poe Museum, 1914 East Main Street, Richmond VA 23223 (1-888-213-2763; www.poemuseum.org)

St. John's Church, 2319 East Broad Street, Richmond, VA 23223 (804-649-0263; www.historicstjohnschurch.org)

Virginia State Capitol, 1000 Bank Street, Richmond, VA 23219 (804-698-1788; www.virginiacapitol.gov)

Monumental Church, 1224 East Broad Street, Richmond, VA (www.historicrichmond.com/preservation-monumental.php)

Library of Virginia, 800 East Broad Street, Richmond, VA 23219 (804-692-3500; www.lva.virginia.gov)

⚓ LITERARY LODGING

THE JEFFERSON HOTEL

Virginia's capital city, whose destiny and heritage were largely shaped by Civil War heroes and tobacco barons, overlooks the rock-strewn James River and is home to the AAA Five-Diamond Jefferson Hotel, which tells the city's story like no other.

The hotel was the daring and costly dream of Major Lewis Gintner, one of Richmond's wealthier tobacco barons. He spared no expense in fulfilling his ambitious dream of constructing the city's finest hotel, employing the architectural firm of Carrere and Hastings. He imported items from around the globe, with estimated costs of the hotel exceeding $10 million.

Opening night—Halloween Eve 1895—ushered in a new era in Virginia's capital city. Fancy carriages lined up for miles along Franklin Street, dispatching elegantly attired guests into the hotel. The evening's most coveted social event took place in the Roof Garden, where New York architect Stanford White threw a lavish party for Richmond debutante Irene Langhorne and her dashing fiancé Charles Dana Gibson of Gibson Girl fame. The southern city was transformed overnight from a tired remnant of the Civil War into a symbol of the New South. Following the Gilded Age, the hotel hosted a range of literary guests including Scott and Zelda Fitzgerald and Thomas Wolfe, who stopped in on his train trips from New York.

A member of the National Trust's Historic Hotels of American, the Jefferson holds a striking and commanding statue of Thomas Jefferson sculpted by Edward Valentine in the lobby. The grand staircase that descends from the main lobby to the lower level will remind guests of *Gone with the Wind* with **Lemaire's,** its upscale dining spot, featuring European fare. A small but in-depth History Gallery on the main floor studies details of the hotel's rich past. The Jefferson offers a complimentary car service whereby a driver will take you to destinations within a few miles of the hotel, including the Poe Museum and sites.

Jefferson Hotel, 101 West Franklin Street, Richmond, VA 23220 (804-649-4750; www.jeffersonhotel.com)

⊛ EXCURSIONS AND DIVERSIONS

MUSEUM CITY

Virginia's capital is abundant with first-class museums. And its Civil War connections are unsurpassed: The **Civil War Trail** begins at the **American Civil War Center,** which is housed in the 1861 Tredegar Gun Factory. The three-story center traces the origins of the Civil War and the role Richmond played in the drama. **Hollywood Cemetery** is not only one of the city's most important landmarks but also the site where many Confederate soldiers are interred, including J. E. B. Stuart. The cemetery winds through 135 acres of valleys over hills and offers stunning views of Richmond.

Another exceptional museum to explore is the **Virginia Museum of Fine Arts,** which houses an outstanding collection of art nouveau, art deco, and impressionist paintings; the most eye-catching exhibits may be Paul Mellon's British Sporting Paintings and the museum's stained-glass works. The Fabergé Collection—the largest outside Russia—will reopen in 2015. This collection features imperial Easter eggs, enameled photograph frames, cigarette cases, and delicately designed artifacts by famed court jeweler Peter Carl Fabergé. Plan on spending at least a full day at this outstanding museum. A café, gift shop, and special programs make this one of Richmond's finest cultural venues.

Nearby the **Virginia Historical Museum** tells the "story of Virginia." A Conestoga wagon, vintage Richmond streetcar, buttons from Pocahontas's hat, and original documents and letters associated with Edgar Allan Poe are just a portion of its extensive collection.

Farther afield in Petersburg is another prime Civil War site, the **Petersburg National Battlefield.** Approximately 30 minutes from Richmond is where one of the most pivotal battles of the Civil War took place—the Siege of Petersburg on April 3, 1865. The driving tour includes over 13 sites and three visitors centers along a 33-mile route. An entire day should be devoted to this excursion. At the Eastern Front Center, films and exhibits explain the battle, where more than 70,000 lost their lives. General Grant's headquarters— where he strategically cut off Lee's supply lines—is part of this tour. The fall of Richmond followed six days later, leading to Lee's surrender. On a side note, much of the filming for Steven Spielberg's 2012 film *Lincoln* was shot both in Richmond and at this historic battlefield.

Civil War Trail (www.virginia.org/CivilWarTrails)

American Civil War Center, 500 Tredegar Street, Richmond, VA 23219 (804-780-1865; www.tredegar.org)

Hollywood Cemetery, 412 South Cherry Street, Richmond, VA 23220 (804-644-7345; www.hollywoodcemetery.org)

Virginia Museum of Fine Arts, 200 North Boulevard, Richmond, VA 23220 (804-340-1400; www.vmfa.state.va.us)

Virginia Historical Museum, 428 North Boulevard, Richmond, VA 23220 (804-358-4901; www.vahistorical.org)

Petersburg National Battlefield, 1539 Hickory Hill Road, Petersburg, VA 23803 (804-732-3531; www.nps.gov/pete)

Virginia Tourism Corp., 901 E. Byrd Street, Richmond, VA 23219 (804-545-5500, www.vatc.org)

Ꮽ Schuyler

> *On the day before Thanksgiving the Spencer clan began to gather. It was a custom that at this time during the year the nine sons would come together in New Dominion. On Thanksgiving Eve they would celebrate their reunion with food and drink and talk.*
>
> —EARL HAMNER JR., *Spencer's Mountain*

TRAVELING INTO CHARLOTTESVILLE on Route 29 from Lynchburg, you will find the tiny village of Schuyler tucked away in the Piedmont region of the Blue Ridge Mountains. This is where Earl Hamner, author and creator of the popular television series *The Waltons,* spent his childhood.

The Waltons was based on Depression-era Virginia, as was Hamner's novel *Spencer's Mountain*—his heartwarming story about growing up in Virginia in a family with limited resources but genuine love. The main character John Boy, based on Hamner, told the story of his Virginia youth and the close-knit family's struggles, achievements, and daily life.

Walton's Mountain Museum is located in the Schuyler elementary school, from which Hamner graduated in 1940, and travels back in time to 1930s rural Virginia. Exhibits re-create the TV series sets. Ike Godsey's store, John Boy's room, and the kitchen where so many events took place are on view, along with Hamner's writing awards, including an Emmy. Photographs of his family are placed next to the cast members who represented them. A 30-minute video prior to your tour features Hamner along with the stars of the show. Admission proceeds go toward a college scholarship fund for promising Schuyler students.

Walton's Mountain Museum, 6484 Rockfish River Road, Schuyler, VA 22969 (434-831-2000; www.waltonmuseum.org)

ACKNOWLEDGMENTS

FIRST OFF this book was a subject close to my heart and began several years ago after visiting Thomas Wolfe's home in Asheville. I felt his story along with those of the other writers mentioned in the book was a story worth telling. My desire was to add another dimension on this literary journey to these literary icons who transformed the American literary landscape.

Visitors Guide to the Literary South would never have seen the light of day without the encouragement and enthusiasm of my editor, Kermit Hummel of The Countryman Press. From the very beginning he recognized the book's merit and more than anyone involved with the book urged me to continue writing and working on the book when I became frustrated and exhausted from the endeavor. His continual trust in my editorial effort and to "press on" became a very important component in completing the book. There were days when I felt overwhelmed by the subject matter but Kermit insisted I stay the creative course believing that this book would stand apart from others in taking travelers on this literary journey.

I also have to thank the many libraries, in particular the University of North Carolina's Wilson Library and Duke University's Perkins Library, along with the Durham Public Library Southwest Branch for their ongoing efforts in research. The front desk staff at the Durham Library Southwest Branch was exceptional on every level in letting this writer day after day continue the process of piecing together the chapters. Archivists and historians at the various sites also proved invaluable when research began. Special mention should be given to Christian Edwards at the Thomas Wolfe Memorial in Asheville, who provided me with a wealth of information on his life in the Old Kentucky Home; Journalist David Page for his extensive knowledge on F. Scott Fitzgerald; Jennifer Crisp of Richmond's Jefferson Hotel, who allowed me spend several days researching Edgar Allan Poe's life in that city; the Henry Plant Museum in Tampa for their detailed information on Stephen Crane; and the Atlanta History Center for their assistance on Margaret Mitchell's life. Other important mentions have to include the Louisiana State Capitol and Louisiana State University for their Robert Penn Warren material; the Tennessee Williams Literary Festival for providing me with a wealth of material on Williams as well as archival photographs; Louisville's Seelbach Hotel for allowing me to visit and explore the F. Scott Fitzgerald connection to the hotel; the University of Virginia for their insight into both William Faulkner and Edgar Allan Poe's life at the university; Charleston, South Carolina, for material on DuBose Heyward and *Porgy & Bess,* as well as the Francis Marion Hotel for allowing me to explore Charleston; and the Marjorie Kinnan Rawlings home for pertinent details about her life in Cross Creek, Florida. The Oxford Convention & Visitors Bureau for their in-depth information on William Faulkner and Loyola University in New Orleans for their Walker Percy information. Special mention should also be given to the Thomas Wolfe Memorial in Asheville and Margaret Mitchell's Atlanta apartment—those landmarks inspired me from the beginning to write this book and paved the way for the other writers' landmarks throughout the South, to Stephen Crane and F. Scott Fitzgerald, whose youthful photographs on my desk guided me throughout this writing process. To Ibby and John Henry whose bright and beautiful smiles will never be forgotten. And last but certainly not least to Steven Foxwell, my trusted and enthusiastic traveling companion and an extraordinary explorer who spent as much time in the library fact-checking and putting together material as I did, and for his enthusiasm in being as excited as I was in writing this book after ten hours at the library! Finally, to all of the writers mentioned in the book whose illuminating lives inspired me to keep at it and remain true to the heart of the book in telling their particular story on this enthralling literary journey.

BIBLIOGRAPHY

Black, Stephen A. *Eugene O'Neill: Beyond Mourning and Tragedy.* New Haven, CT: Yale University Press, 1999.

Faulkner, William. *New Orleans Sketches.* New York: Random House, 1958.

Fitzgerald, F. Scott. *The Great Gatsby.* Cambridge, UK: Cambridge University Press, 1991.

Grisham, John. *The Firm.* New York: Doubleday, 1991.

Hyland, William G. *George Gershwin.* Westport, CT: Praeger, 2003.

Jablonski, Edward. *Gershwin: A Biography.* New York: Doubleday, 1987.

Leverich, Lyle. *Tom: The Unknown Tennessee Williams.* New York: Crown, 1994.

Marrs, Suzanne. *Eudora Welty: A Biography.* Orlando, FL: Harcourt, 2005.

Meyers, Jeffrey. *Scott Fitzgerald: A Biography.* New York: HarperCollins, 1994.

Milford, Nancy. *Zelda: A Biography.* New York: Harper & Row, 1970.

Oates, Stephen B. *William Faulkner: The Man and the Artist; A Biography.* New York: Harper & Row, 1987.

Prigozy, Ruth. *F. Scott Fitzgerald.* London and New York: Penguin and Overlook Press, 2002.

Reynolds, Michael. *The Young Hemingway.* New York: W. W. Norton, 1986.

Shields, Charles J. *Mockingbird: A Portrait of Harper Lee.* New York: Henry Holt, 2006.

Welty, Eudora. *Delta Wedding.* New York: Harcourt Brace, 1946.

Wolfe, Thomas. *The Hills Beyond.* New York: Harper & Brothers, 1941.

————. *Look Homeward, Angel.* New York: Scribner's, 1929.

INDEX